I pray this uplifts yo

— [signature]

SELF-DECLARATIONS
40 Day Devotional

Derrell L. Dean

Scriptures are from the *Holy Bible,* New King James Version© 1982 by Thomas Nelson Inc. Used by permission. All rights reserved.

Published in the United States by CreateSpace Inc.

Library of Congress Cataloging-in- Publication Data

Dean, Derrell L.

Self-Declarations: 40 Day Devotional/Derrell L. Dean

Pages cm

ISBN: 1533332665 (electronic)
ISBN-13: 978-1533332660 (hardcover)

DEDICATION

This devotional book is dedicated to my grandmother, Mrs. Mary E. Strange-Dirton, my grandparents, the late Mr. and Mrs. James Odell and Mamie Reid-Dean, and the late Mr. Henry Dirton. Your blood runs through my veins and I'm thankful for your wisdom and life lessons. To my parents, Mr. and Mrs. Jerry and Linda Dean-- your support and encouragement in my life has been monumental for who I am and I'm forever grateful. Thank you for raising my brothers and I with such strength, humility, faith and love.

To my gifted brothers, Jerrell and Lenell Dean-being your brother and watching the impactful things you do individually has been a blessing. To the Dean and Dirton Families, I love you all and I'm glad to have such a blessed family tree. I pray for you all daily. To my church families, Fairfield United Methodist Church and Long Branch Baptist Church- thank you for sharing your lives with mine. I'm forever humbled to worship God and walk this road of life with you and I love you all.

Thank you indeed!!

CONTENTS

PREFACE

One may ask, what is the strength in the "I am" declarations? The power of these declarations, are not that they are statements for your future state, they are declarations of your present state, which will propel you into the blessings of your future. When you know who you are and who you belong to, it gives you the assurance and confidence that He who has called you, before you entered into your mother's womb, is also the One who will keep you during all trials, tribulations, or persecutions you will encounter. The blessings of "I am" declarations are that you are walking, talking, and living in the same language that God himself spoke:

I AM WHO I AM. (Exodus 3:14)

I AM Jehovah Rapha the Lord who heals you. (Exodus 15:26)

I Am Alpha and Omega. (Revelations 22:13)

I AM the Way the Truth and the Life. (John 14:6)

I AM the Good Shepherd. (John 10:11)

I AM the Bread of Life. (John 6:35)

I AM He who is, who was, and is to come, the Almighty. (Rev. 1:8)

As you speak your "I am" declarations, know that you do not speak them with pride or arrogance, you speak them in faith, confidence, and knowledge that the Great "I AM" has caused you to be who YOU ARE.

-Pastor Sean Dogan

SELF –DECLARATIONS
40 Day Devotional

10|13|17

Day 1

"I AM A DISCIPLE"

"So likewise, whoever of you does not forsake all that he has cannot be My disciple.

-Luke 14:33

I very vividly remember my collegiate years as being a time of much studying and testing. As a history major, I had to be purposeful in what I did. That's not to say I always made the right decision but I had to get to a place of devotion in my studies if I wanted to successfully see and obtain my degree. For me, that meant putting my personal agenda to the side, to give myself completely to my educational work.

This method of putting away our plans for a new assignment even makes its way into the church, as well as other arenas. In order to effectively be a great choir member or singer, one must firstly be a great student of all things musically related. Great singers spend time with music. They develop their sound and by listening and predicting changes in the dynamics of the music, they become more inclined in their endeavors.

For today's declaration Jesus proposed such a theme to his disciples that he called. In Luke 14:33 NKJV he spoke to them saying "So likewise, whoever of you does not forsake all that he has cannot be My disciple." If His disciples were consumed with where they were they wouldn't fully be able to step into their future. Their future was essentially to be His voices throughout Judea and everywhere God's Spirit would lead them.

Luke 9:1-6 details Him sending them out. It reads, "Then He called His twelve disciples together and gave them power and authority over all demons and to cure diseases. He sent them to preach the kingdom of God and to heal the sick. And He then said to them, "Take nothing for the journey, neither staffs nor bag nor bread nor money; and do not have two tunics apiece. Whatever house you enter, stay there, and from there depart. And whoever will not receive you, when you go out of that city, shake off the very dust from your feet as a testimony against them." So they departed and went through the towns, preaching the gospel and healing everywhere."

My friends, you and I are not called as disciples for a popularity contest. It's not for self-esteem or special seating. Disciples aren't disciples because all their friends are. They are because they have a desire to be led and covered in the way that they should go. Disciples are synonymous with a student. Students never get to a point of being greater than their teacher. It is by humbleness and self-denial that students rise to greatness. Disciples attain knowledge, understanding and are equipped to handle what lies ahead of them with humility, compassion and strength. To be a disciple it costs you everything.

Today's Declaration Challenge: Disciples were not always well received everywhere they went. Be challenged to stay in God's word and let his word stay in you. Know that your purpose is greater than what you see. Even when disappointment tries to set you back, you have a command as a disciple to dust your feet off, square your shoulders and press on. Discipline your thoughts to be cross-centered today. Be challenged enough to keep learning and renewing your mind to believe God for the impossible. You may be the vessel God uses to draw those around you to Christ. Today declare that "**I am a disciple**."

My Conviction

As a teacher I must Study to show myself approved! How can I teach what I have not First learned/worthin by Experience or teaching by Holy Spirit

10|13|07

Day 2

"I AM ROYALTY"

"Now the Lord said to Samuel, "How long will you mourn for Saul, seeing I have rejected him from reigning over Israel? Fill your horn with oil, and go: I am sending you to Jesse the Bethlehemite. For I have provided Myself a king among his sons."

-1 Samuel 16:1

There's a king or a queen in you. When you purpose in your heart to realize the depths of your potential, you don't desire to live any less than the king or queen that you are. You may not physically grace the halls of a palace but that does not negate nor diminish your royalty with God. The idea of you being a king or queen is ultimately a conception that there is greatness in you. It is possible that others will see the king in you before you will.

Personal moment: My grandfather would take my brothers and I to Sunday school before church when we were young. Our classes would then disperse into the youth group from the adults. The youth class would study the assigned lesson and then we would merge back into the adult class and present what we learned. My brothers and I would always go back and forth as to who would give the lesson each time. It was in those moments that my grandfather would see a preacher in one of us, that we wouldn't necessarily see in ourselves. We would later find out that he had a conversation with our teacher instructing her to "make a preacher" out of one of us. Though she would instruct us, it would be God that would do the calling and leading and years later I would step into ministry much to my own amazement.

God called David in a way that he wasn't expecting so to speak. David was actively shepherding his father's sheep not thinking about the palace. The prophet Samuel would be led to Bethlehem to seek Jesse and to anoint one of his sons as king of the Israelites. Samuel met with a challenge when Jesse passed 7 of his sons before him and neither of them was chosen. God had to instruct Samuel and say "Do not look at his appearance or at his physical stature, because I have refused him. For the Lord does not see as man sees; for man looks at the outward appearance, but the Lord looks at the heart" (1 Samuel 16:7).

It is the qualities of your heart that make you a leader. Does that mean that you must be perfect? No it certainly does not. It means that in order to be a king or queen in your environments you must possess a character that is strong enough to be humble. When you know that you're a king or queen, you don't consume your energy in things that are futile and immature. Be encouraged because what man denies, God approves.

It is symbolic that the very people that are most rejected are the ones that God puts his seal of royalty on. David, a shepherd boy, who had no ties to the kingdom, was exalted to the office because of the heart he possessed. We see David's life even as a precursor for the life of Jesus. Jesus, though he was from the seed of David, He also was refused as king when the news of His birth spread that He would be the king of kings. Herod sought to take Jesus' life early on and we see that rejection throughout His later years. I say that to say that when God has assigned royalty and power to your life, the authority only works for you. Others may try their best to interfere or deter your purpose but when God has designed you for something greater, their attacks won't work.

Today's Declaration Challenge: I challenge you to believe in your fullest potential. Believe in yourself again. Carry yourself with a presence of grace and authority. I challenge you to declare that there is more to you than what you see. Look yourself in the mirror and declare **"I am royalty."**

Day 3

"I AM AT PEACE"

"Peace I leave with you, My peace I give to you; not as the world gives do I give to you. Let not your heart be troubled, neither let it be afraid."

-John 14:27

The idea or concept of peace and having peace is relative to some and foreign to others. Peace is something we all desire whether we realize it or not. In our search to have it, many times we dismiss ourselves from the norm to look for it. We spend money on vacations where we literally vacate the premises of our daily walk to an unknown or unfamiliar place searching for peace. We look for it in a sunrise, a sunset or on the beachside. It's amazing the great lengths we will go to attain peace.

The Lord himself proclaimed that he would leave "peace" with his disciples. It was to be a gift from Him, in the midst of a world of trouble. He knew all too well what was set before him and those with Him but even still he wanted them to have and receive the peace within their hearts. In actuality, peace should be within our hearts no matter where we are.

This was a message that the Apostle Paul conveyed to the

Philippians in his writings to them. He tells them "Be anxious for nothing but in everything by prayer and supplication, with thanksgiving, let your requests be made known to God' and the peace of God, which surpasses all understanding will guard your hearts and minds through Christ Jesus (Philippians 4:6-7). He gives them notice that peace will secure you.

I've come to discover that peace will keep your heart and your mind from the ways of this world. It is possible to have peace and be amassed by opposition. It is possible to operate and function while being surrounded by your enemies. When you make an internal decision to remain at peace, the people and things around you cannot set you back. If you're up against a layoff, foreclosure, loss of a loved one, or pending bills, whatever you do, don't lose your peace. It will be the foundation of your success and advancement. It will settle you every day that you live.

If you lose your peace, you may lose your security and stability. Life will quickly show you when your peace is gone. It is hard to reclaim it once it is lost. You can receive it back but it takes time. You may be in that place today and if you are don't beat yourself up about it. This is not the end of your story. Don't let the problems of this life cause you to miss the promises of your next place in God. God then will have to lead you by His Spirit to a place of solitude or prayer to get it back.

Let peace be your lot today. If you need more of it, I pray

that God sends you exactly what you need for what you have to handle. Peace will be the anchor for the toughest of times and it will bless you indeed.

Today's Declaration Challenge: I challenge you on this day to let peace find you even in the most trying of times. Let God's peace calm your heart and mind and bring clarity to your thoughts. When others expect the worst of you, show them the best of you by walking, talking and living in peace. Declare to yourself today that **"I am at peace."**

Day 4

"I AM A WINNER"

"For though I am free from all men, I have made myself a servant to all that I might win the more…"

-1 Corinthians 9:19

For every winner, there is some type of failure in their history. There was a moment of trial or pain that caused a setback in their progress. That type of setback motivated them to try harder, to apply again and at least make another attempt. It was with a determined heart and settled mind that the goal was reached and the battle was won.

Our salvation works in that same manner. In the midst of our own failures and attempts to do things our way and live life as we know it, Christ compelled us. He saved us from the cares of this world and ignited a passion in us by His Spirit to always win. As you go throughout your day today, I pray that this same passion to win will be with you as you go.

The Apostle Paul was such a winner in that he sought to win others for the cause of Christ by his servitude and example. He entered into his missionary journeys with the mentality to say "I am a winner." In 1 Corinthians 9:22-23 he states "to the weak I became as weak, that I might win the weak. I have become all things to all men that I might by all means save some. Now this I do for the gospel's sake, that I may be partaker of it with you."

Paul made it his business to go after souls. For much of the New Testament writings that are attributed to him, he wanted his life to be an example to the other believers and even those he sought to convert. After his conversion in Acts 9 on the Damascus Road, he would go on to compel many others to the cause of Christ and salvation therein.

In our lives, do we make such a stance our business and desire to win souls today? Are we really sharing this gospel to those that we see from day to day? Can Christ come into our conversations with family and friends? Have we committed our lives to pull others from the grips of this world or do we assume they already have it together?

I've come to discover one truth about winning souls for the Lord and it is that many times it's not always our words that pull them to him but our actions. Words have power to draw people to Him but that adage is true that "actions do speak louder than words." The way we present ourselves and our overall demeanor makes a difference to those that we meet. If I strike you as standoffish and condescending in the manner that I speak to you, you would quickly dismiss anything I would have to say. If I display my humanity, humbleness and grace towards you, then you would be more prone to listen to my witness. Our lives are many times the only examples of Christ people will see.

By taking on the character of a winner, I agree to be determined in my approach to ministry, in my relationships and fellowships. I agree to be approachable to those around me, not to where I compromise the God in me but I am able to meet them where they are and help usher them to where they will be. I've discovered that it's not the extravagant things that win people but sometimes it's the little things or even foolish things that help them reach their destiny. Your smile may be the smile to save someone on the brink of causing harm to themselves or others.

Today's Declaration Challenge: Let us be challenged today to "win" others for Christ. Be challenged to point others to a relationship with the one that never fails. It may not be welcomed in every arena to push Christ but let your life lift up the name of the Lord in truth and love and watch God's Spirit draw others unto Himself. Declare today **"I am a winner."**

Day 5

"I AM FREE"

"Then Jesus said to those Jews who believed Him, "If you abide in My word, you are My disciples indeed. And you shall know the truth, and the truth shall make you free."

-John 8:31-32

For many, freedom is not free. It comes with a cost. As believers, our freedom came with a price that was only paid by Christ' shed blood on Calvary. Freedom or the state of being free must happen in the natural or your physical surroundings but it must also happen in our minds internally. If anyone has ever been bound physically, they will witness to you that the opportunity to be free again was something they truly desired. For many freedom in the mind is something that we all should long for.

I've often said in my preaching ministry, that if anything has your mind it has you. If we can all be honest, we've all had moments where we felt our minds were out of control. It was at those times that we needed God through His Son to bring peace, clarity and freedom to us. Jesus brought the truth to those around him in essence to free them from lives that were bound to the ways of this world. He let them know that God's word would keep them connected to the source as disciples. Disciples are knowledgeable of the truth and by that truth they are free. We are challenged today to not entangle ourselves with anything or anyone that will keep us bound.

Be free even from your own insecurities. Many times we personally hold ourselves down from doing powerful things by living with self doubt and a lack of confidence. That can be detrimental to your growth and development. When you talk yourself out of many things, you'll never grasp the concept of fully giving yourself to anything and seeing it come to completion. That's a form of self-bondage.

If Christ set me free by my belief in Him, then I truly find freedom in Him and not the ways of this world. Romans 8:2 states that "For the law of the Spirit of life in Christ Jesus has made me free from the law of sin and death." I now live under another law and that is the law of the Spirit. Yes I take residence in the state and country of my choosing where I abide by that laws of this land but yet I have another law that I live under as well. This law not only governs me physically but mentally. This law opens my eyes to see God's glory in those around me and the power of what he will do for His own.

Freedom through Christ should not be forsaken. If you are free and you know what it feels like to be released from bondage whether it was physical or emotional, you are called to do all within your power to help someone else experience that same freedom. Let them know of the power of God's Spirit. "Now the

Lord is the Spirit; and where the Spirit of the Lord is there is liberty" (2 Corinthians 3:17). Let the Lord's Spirit set you free.

Today's Declaration Challenge: Be challenged to walk in confidence today. When you know you have the goods and what it takes to make it, don't count yourself out. Raise your hand as a sign of your liberty. Be free to live again. Enjoy this life. Go after the thing you put away years ago. Be free to find your way. It is my prayer that today you will proudly declare **"I am free."**

Day 6

"I AM DELIVERED"

"The righteous cry out, and the Lord hears, and delivers them out of all their troubles."

-Psalm 34:17

I often say that freedom can't come in our lives alone. For that very reason, the declaration from yesterday goes closely in correlation with today's declaration from my beliefs.

Freedom or the state of being free in my opinion must not solely be the end of our story when we find ourselves in various situations. Freedom has to be accompanied by deliverance. Essentially freedom only looses you from the bonds that hold you down but the spirit of deliverance doesn't allow you to go back. Many times we're free from some things but not delivered but the two must go hand and hand.

It was after Moses had led the Israelites of the Old Testament out of slavery in Egypt that they began to show how free they truly were. In Exodus 16:3, they began to speak out to Moses "And the children of Israel said to them, "Oh that we had died by the hand of the Lord in the land of Egypt, when we sat by the pots of meat and when we ate bread to the full! For you have brought us out into this wilderness to kill this whole assembly with hunger;" They were free physically from the grips and commands of Egyptian captivity but yet were not delivered in their minds. God had to speak to Moses to assure them that He would provide bread from heaven and water when they so needed it.

God would assure them of their freedom, deliverance and dependence on Him by saying "I have heard the complaints of the children of Israel. Speak to them, saying, 'At twilight you shall eat meat, and in the morning you shall be filled with bread. And you shall know that I am the Lord your God (Exodus 16:12)." Deliverance is at its truest form when we no longer desire to go back to where we used to be.

If you find yourself in a predicament, problem or circumstance that you cannot get out of, do not fret. You could possibly be on the other side of your greatest obstacle but mentally struggle due to a fear of what's ahead of you or if you will have what it takes to carry on. Maybe you need deliverance from your own ways and the actions of your hands. There's good news today that not only will God free you from where you are but He'll deliver you from the idea that where you were was your resting place.

"Many are the afflictions of the righteous but the Lord delivers him out of them all (Psalm34:19)." In all of our afflictions, God still delivers. He still brings us out. He still carries us over every snare of the enemy. He still grants us a chance to experience full deliverance.

Today's Declaration Challenge: I challenge you today to let the Lord guide you out of anything that has you bound. Let him deliver you from even your dependence on what used to sustain you. Be challenged to let Him deliver you to your blessed place. When the Lord delivers you, there is no question it was the Lord that brought you to where you are. Let your voice be heard declaring **"I am delivered."**

"I AM FORGIVEN"

"And be kind to one another, tenderhearted, forgiving one another even as God in Christ forgave you."

-Ephesians 4:32

Every day that we live we have the power to make sound decisions. Though we have the option to do right, we also have the propensity and capability to do wrong. No matter how saintly or blessed you and I may appear on the exterior to be, we all can admittedly say that we have messed up. We all have fallen short of God's glory in our lifetimes. It's a fact of our existence.

It was at an early age that I gave my heart to the Lord. I can remember the overwhelming feelings of remorse and guilt for everything that I had done wrong in my 18 years of life. It was a tearful time but a joyous moment as I asked the Lord into my heart by the prayer of confession. I was forgiven by God but was still challenged to forgive myself for what I had done and to forgive any offenders along the way.

The Apostle Paul spoke to the church at Ephesus on this issue and reminded them of this very thing saying "And be kind to one another, tenderhearted, forgiving one another even as God in

Christ forgave you (Ephesians 4:32)." Forgiveness allows me to navigate through the pain, past hurts or offenses from yesterday. If I need to forgive someone, the forgiveness is not to make them feel better about themselves but rather to release the hurt of the offense off of myself. It allows me to press forward toward a better future. Though they may be comforted, forgiving them empowers me.

I am not ignorant to believe that all of the issues of yesterday or years past can be wiped away overnight. I do believe however that those same difficulties can be healed and brought to some level of closure. If you're in the position to make a situation such as this better today, choose to do so, not to satisfy your present but to move into your tomorrow with peace and some level of understanding.

As a believer, we should never hold our heads so far down with the weight of our wrongs that we neglect the forgiveness that we received. When you know God has forgiven you, your soul should move from being downtrodden to being lifted up towards our God of grace. With forgiveness, I can walk in power and the boldness of God.

Paul writes, "In Him we have redemption through His blood, the forgiveness of sins, according to the riches of His grace (Ephesians 1:7)." As you go about this day, you may see someone that acquainted themselves with you in years past or go around places from ages long past but be encouraged. Choose to not go back to a place of discouragement. Never allow the thoughts of others that knew you from your past to dictate who you are in your future. Permit yourself to forgive yourself. Once you can look yourself in the eye, remind others that you are not who you used to be. You don't wear those old clothes of bondage and pain anymore.

Today's Declaration Challenge: I challenge you to let forgiveness be your stay. Forgive those offenders for what they did to you but also forgive them for the things that did not happen, that they were not able to fulfill. Forgive yourself from your own wrong decisions. Don't let your yesterday ruin your tomorrow. Today boldly declare **"I am forgiven."**

Day 8

"I AM VICTORIOUS"

"So Joshua did as Moses said to him, and fought with Amalek; And Moses, Aaron, and Hur went up to the top of the hill. And so it was, when Moses held up his hand that Israel prevailed; and when he let down his hand, Amalek prevailed."

-Exodus 17:10-11

At nearly every athletic event in the world, the winner is very evident above the ones that have lost in the competition. The victor distinctively does something that their opponent isn't able to do and that is lifting their hands in victory.

The lifting of the arms is synonymous with the act of prevailing over one's competition. In the culture of the Christian church, many believers will readily lift their hands in the spirit of intense worship, in signs of agreement as well as surrender to the Lord. These are characteristics of lives that are reliant on the Lord to be their help.

The children of Israel found themselves in moments where they also needed the Lord's help. The Amalekites rose up against them in battle but Joshua led them on the field. Exodus 17:11 reads, "And so it was, when Moses held up his hand, that Israel prevailed; and when he let down his hand, Amalek prevailed." The text would go on to say that even in Moses' fatigue that Aaron and Hur helped him by propping his arms upward until the victory was won. What a great display of victory!! What an awesome example of triumph!!

It's very noteworthy that Moses had help in his distress to his victory. It was with the assistance of Aaron and Hur that the Israelites were successful. Who's on your team today? Who will assist you without being formally invited to do so but just because they believe in you? Who helps you not for accolades or applause but because it's in their heart to do so? Who will help you achieve victory in your relationships and business endeavors through encouragement?

Any real champion knows that it wasn't solely the work of their own hands that brought them to where they are. They had a coach, an encourager, a guide, a friend or mentor to help them make it. The coach understands that when the mentee wins, we all win because it was a collective effort. I suggest to you that if someone is close to you but not propelling you to your next place of victory that they are just dead weight. Let them go. Give them their walking papers. Not only did Moses and the Israelites have Joshua, Aaron and Hur at a pivotal time but they all had God on their side. True victories come from minds that are purposed to win. They were purposed to keep their arms lifted. Victory belonged to them. In that same manner, you and I have victory as children of the king. When you rise in the morning, tell yourself I've got victory. When I praise God in spite of what I see, I've got victory. When I endure what others gave up on, I'm on my way to victory. Being victorious has nothing to do with arrogance but everything to do with consistency. I choose to be victorious in my walk by consistently choosing to press on.

Today's Declaration Challenge: I challenge you to never neglect the importance of lifting your hands up to a strong and powerful God. You may be up against giants financially, emotionally or spiritually but don't let the looks of others change your posture towards God. Be encouraged to know that with your hands lifted up, God's Spirit will meet you where you are and the victory shall be yours. Lift your hands and gladly declare **"I am victorious."**

"I AM RESTORED"

"Brethren, if a man is overtaken in any trespass, you who are spiritual restore such a one in a spirit of gentleness; considering yourself lest you also be tempted."

-Galatians 6:1

Our automobiles will go as far as we need them to go as long as they have what they need to run efficiently. When the gas is not on empty and the maintenance on it is kept in tune, it will carry on for many miles and years. The moment the maintenance fails, the battery is low or even the gas is on empty, it completely lets you know by not running smoothly or working properly at all. At that moment, the vehicle needs to be "restored" to its proper glory.

My friends, our lives are like that especially when we use our entire being in service to others, our responsibilities and obligations. Once the workday comes to an end, the commute home is finished, the kids are fed, bills are paid, family is cared for, church work is complete, the sick and shut in are cared for and our needs are met, we need restoration. We need it because in most cases we'll go to bed only to wake up and do the same thing all over again. The cycle will continue. No matter who we are, none of us can operate on "E" or empty and be successful.

Restoration can come in many ways. One may find it on the beautiful beaches of your favorite getaway, on a hiking expedition, or in a peaceful cabin site. You can even find restoration through the power of soothing music. One thing that is sure and that is our spirit needs to be restored. A great disservice is done to you when you don't allow yourself to be restored. Now if you're not doing anything you may not need restoration as much as someone who is active. If we miss the opportunities for restoration we forfeit the blessing of God pouring back into us by His Spirit.

Restoration is not just for the tired but it's also for the broken. Galatians 6:1 reads "If a man is overtaken in any trespass you who are spiritual restore such a one in a spirit of gentleness." Today you may be in a good place on your journey. You may run across someone who visibly is not in the same condition as you. Their struggle may not even be spoken of but evident to the natural eye. You have a right as a believer to pray with them until times get better. You have a responsibility to show them love until they are restored. Help someone have the testimony of David that "He restores my soul" (Psalm 23:3).

If you've received restoration at any moment in your life, you should desire to see others receive it as well. You may need restoration in your family structure based on offenses that happened years ago. It's okay to be away from the situation a while until you get yourself together. With that said, the only way to make the situation better or restored is when you are able to face what you need to fix. You cannot resolve a matter that you're not willing to face. Confront the problem. Express how it made you feel. Admit your issue and seek to live in a more excellent and restored way. Restoration won't always happen overnight but if the door is open it will eventually come your way.

Today's Declaration Challenge: Be encouraged to know that someone is praying you back to your rightful place. I challenge to set aside time for YOU (your goals, your health, your vision and peace of mind). Let God restore your soul to a place of fullness. Proudly declare **"I am restored."**

Day 10

"I AM A WORK IN PROGRESS"

"Being confident of this very thing, that He who has begun a good work in you will complete it until the day of Jesus Christ;"

-Philippians 1:6

At any given time, signs of progress are often all around us. Sometimes we see progress due to regression such as on a road or highway riddled with potholes and broken places. Progress happens when a college student finishes that last exam and walks across that stage to receive that degree. We see it when persons that were once debilitated by a sickness, accident or disease regain some level of normalcy and strength. It happens all around us.

I'll never forget as I began to drive that I would have the pleasure of driving my grandmother around to the places she wanted to go in the city of Greenville, SC. She would look at buildings and landscapes around us and say "that wasn't here when I was a little girl. In fact, none of those buildings were here when I was young. There's something changing all the time." I remember that fondly because she was not only recalling moments in her lifetime but teaching me a lesson that in order for some things to grow there must be change.

Our lives should always be progressing from one area to another. We should always be able to testify that we've come "a mighty long way" (as I've often heard growing up in church) from where we started from. The truth of the matter is progress is also uncomfortable. That is the case because things get moved around, shifted and torn apart when true progress happens. If your progress is comfortable to you, then maybe you're not really progressing or growing. Where there's growth, there has to be change.

From the time you and I awoke this morning and by the time we close our eyes to rest at night, we should have done something in that day to bring about some progress in our lives. That progress could be putting additional time in on a job, completing an educational project to advance our career goals, or making sure the needs of our families are met. Some works of progress may not always be visible externally but keep making moves. Your progress is not in vain.

Every now and then God takes us down pathways where we must allow self-reconstruction to happen. It's in those moments where He slows us down and allows us to notice our own faults and shortcomings. He'll also put us in uncomfortable situations to remind us that no matter how far we've gone, we still need his help to go even further. He also reminds us that we still have areas within us that aren't perfect.

Paul experienced this firsthand as he wrote to the church at

Philippi from a prison cell. Though I'm sure he was rather grateful at what God permitted him to do since becoming a Christian but still somewhat defeated at the same time while sitting in prison. It is possible to have made progress but still feel incomplete. That is natural. It is possible to make moves and still feel unaccomplished. Don't get discouraged today if you feel this way. This is a sign that God is not through with you yet. Even those around you may not recognize your growth and will try to hold you back by your old nature but don't subject yourself to their inability to recognize the change that has come your way. If nobody else sees it, you should still be able to witness to your own growth.

Paul spoke in Philippians 1:6 saying "being confident of this very thing, that He who has begun a good work in you will complete it until the day of Jesus Christ." If God brought you to this moment, He will let you see the end of it. He will finish the work He started in you. He will shape your ways, your attitudes and the direction He wants for you to go. If you're like myself, you will readily witness that you have some things that you need the Lord to finish. I know that's my story because if I try to finish it, I'll leave something out. If I try to finish all that God has for me, I'll make a mistake but if He does it, I know it will be done. When God gets done with you and I, we will have everything we need. When God finishes something in our lives, it's full and complete.

Today's Declaration Challenge: Be challenged to know that your story is still being written. Don't allow yesterday's problems to stop today's promise towards tomorrow's potential. Don't park the car of your life in anything that stops your progress. When others see you and state that you seem different simply lift your voice and declare to them that **"I am a work in progress."**

Day 11

"I AM DETERMINED"

"And he sought to see who Jesus was, but could not because of the crowd, for he was of short stature. So he ran ahead and climbed up into a sycamore tree to see Him, for He was going to pass that way. And when Jesus came to the place, He looked up and saw him, and said to him, "Zacchaeus, make haste and come down, for today I must stay at your house."

-Luke 19:3-5

In order to get anything done or accomplished in this world you have to be determined. This is true for any area whether it be civic, public, private, spiritual or the professional world. Determined people have made an internal choice to finish whatever they've started regardless of the circumstances that they may be in.

Completing assignments either on the job, in school or even personally, require a great deal of determination in order to receive commendation for your labor. A child that is learning to walk must have that same tenacity or determination even though their steps may be wobbly at first. The more they fall, get back up again and continue to put one foot in front of the other, the smoother those steps become. A mind that is determined is not easily swayed by the opinions of doubters or those that aren't able to perceive what you've purposed in your heart to do.

Zacchaeus in the Bible had a determined mind himself in the city of Jericho when he heard that Jesus was passing through the city. Luke 19:3-4 reads "And he sought to see who Jesus was, but could not because of the crowd, for he was of short stature so he ran ahead and climbed up into a sycamore tree to see Him, for He was going to pass that way." Though Zacchaeus was shorter than most, he would not be denied the opportunity of seeing Jesus for himself. His mind was made up to do whatever he needed to do to make that happen, even if it meant getting above the crowd.

I submit unto you that sometimes you have to do things in an unorthodox manner or non-traditional way to get things done. Sometimes that means long hours, extensive training, and many times the long route to your destination. When you are determined it matters not how you get to where you're going but that you get there at all.

We also see determination in Genesis 11 when the people of the earth came together to build the Tower of Babel. God himself spoke and said "Indeed the people are one and they all have one language, and this is what they begin to do; now nothing that they propose to do will be withheld from them (Genesis 11:6)." The people were so determined that even God saw their plans and saw the nature of their heart and realized that nothing could be kept from a determined group. He would then confuse their language because their intentions weren't pure. God wanted them to spread out and inhabit the earth but they wanted to gather together against His word.

What's your determination today? Is it to be successful? Is it to reach major goals or prove others wrong? Could it be to promote Jesus wherever you go? Is it to finish a standing project from your heart to bless others? Are you determined to become more settled and financially fit? The better question may be can the people around you see your determination for what you do or do they see a defeated, unmotivated character? Whatever you're determined to do make sure it's done from the right spirit.

Today's Declaration Challenge: I challenge you to let determination guide your tasks and assignments to the end today. Let the spirit of determination keep your mind stable even around opposition. Remain determined to go all the way. Be purposeful today to have the mind of Zacchaeus, that you will do what you will to ensure you see the Lord for yourself. Readily declare today that **"I am determined."**

"I AM COMMITTED"

"But Ruth said: Where you die; I will die, and there will I be buried. The Lord do so to me and more also, if anything but death parts you and me." When she saw that she was determined to go with her, she stopped speaking to her."

-Ruth 1:16a-18

It was as my first choir director, Mrs. Arbutis Davis, at Fairfield United Methodist Church in Piedmont SC, prepared myself and all of the other youth choir members for our annual choir anniversaries that I realized I had a calling to fulfill with music and a commitment to uphold. It could have been when we all marched down the aisle, took the choir stand to sing our first song that it hit me that I had to commit my heart to music as long as my voice would sing. It became my first love.

I was committed to it and in essence it was stuck to me throughout my educational pilgrimage as I sang on school choirs. My love for music wasn't going anywhere and neither was I. Though I never boast to be the best at it, I'm glad that it still excites me even now. It gives me great joy to hear great music just like it did on that youth choir many years ago as we would sing "His eye is on the sparrow" to waiting congregations.

Just as I was and still am committed to musical pursuits, there's a joy that we all should find in being committed to any cause, gift, place, career or persons that have come our way. Anything that we love, we will ultimately make time for. Great parents make such commitments when they make the decision to bring forth and raise a child and to shape them into being model citizens. Employees and employers do the same day after day as they seek to complete tasks and serve others by what they produce. They commit themselves to doing great service.

Biblically, Ruth displayed such commitment to her mother-in-law, Naomi. As they both lay to rest their husbands and felt they had nothing else left, Ruth made a choice to commit herself to stay by Naomi's side and not leave her alone. Naomi had also lost another son, who was married to Orpah. Ruth would assure Naomi of her commitment by stating to her "Where you die, I will die, and there will I be buried. The Lord do so to me, and more also if anything but death parts you and me (Ruth1:17)." When Naomi heard this, she didn't question Ruth's commitment towards her any longer and the two journeyed to Bethlehem.

Ruth was no longer bound to Naomi since her husband, Naomi's son had died. She could've gone elsewhere but she committed her heart to Naomi. By right, Ruth could have returned to the place of her origin and her birth family unit. Though she was widowed, she still could have led her life and moved on from losing her husband. That would not be the case for Ruth, even though Orpah left and went back to her native land. Ruth remained with Naomi. Their paths were committed to each other.

Are you truly dedicated to your commitments today? Though we're all guilty of letting some things slide, have you let some things go that God himself ordained for you? Are you committed to those that you see every day? Can your coworkers and friends say that your heart is in what you do? Can your family testify of your commitments on your behalf?

Give yourself fully to what you desire to do. Spend time and make a conscious effort with what you feel committed to and watch the difference it makes in your life. I believe that there are many great blessings that God wants to send our way if we would only remain committed to what He's assigned us to. Committed people tend to reap greater harvests than their peers who are less than committed and focused. Committed people tend to see more results as well versus those that left things undone. Keep your hand on the plow and wait with expectation for the harvest of your labor. It will bless you every time.

Today's Declaration Challenge: Be challenged to stick by your commitments even when the conditions are unfavorable. By doing this God many times has a greater blessing for us when we stay the course. If you struggle with commitments in any way, think of what made you agree to be a part of the thing, the cause or the relationship to begin with. When you know your reason "why" you'll be more inclined to remain faithful. If some things have gotten away from you, it's not the end of the matter. Purpose in your heart today to stand by your assignment and those you love and declare **"I am committed."**

"I AM MORE THAN A CONQUEROR"

"Yet in all these things we are more than conquerors through Him who loved us."

-Romans 8:37

From the moment you awoke this morning, you were given another chance to command and conquer your day. As you drive to your place of employment, run your daily errands, or prepare for upcoming events, deadlines and goals, do it with the overall theme of conquering them all.

Conquering your day happens by making a conscious decision on all things that affect your future and plans. If I desire to conquer the thing that has been a hurdle for me, I make the choice to succeed over it. I do it by practicing my craft until it's no longer a hurdle. You and I know very well of areas that we need to conquer and that if we did so the trajectory of our lives would change.

If managing my food intake is one of my most difficult struggles, at some point I must take ownership of what I'm consuming. Foods that are rich in sugars and fatty ingredients cannot be a part of my daily intake. Sticking to a routine that consists of great choices as well as regularly exercising my body creates that spirit of conquering my body's habits and mannerisms.

Paul takes on the idea that believers actually can be more than a conqueror by having Christ Jesus. "Yet in all these things we are more than conquerors through Him who loved us (Romans 8:37)."

Wait a minute? How can we ultimately be more than a conqueror? A conqueror is one who overcomes an enemy or obstacle, but being more than that says that I'm victorious in every area of my being. As long as I have Christ, I have something that money cannot buy. I have something that schools of learning may not be able to fully teach. I have everything I need to be a conqueror from my rising in the morning until my laying down at night. I have victory in my battles and over everything my enemy has. It's mine and it's mine indeed.

Do you have the character of a conqueror today? Are you empowered to have dominion over what you set out to do? Have you counted yourself out of a situation that God meant for you to conquer? Many times we can have what we say from our mouths but yet we talk and think ourselves out of many great things. It's not by the big moves that we become more than conquerors but many times it's the small steps that lead to great advances and distances on our journeys.

Today's Declaration Challenge: Seek to conqueror every facet of this day. I dare you to have the audacity to let nothing stop you today. Conquer your actions, the places that you typically would go and your habits. Conquer your attitude and the way you respond to those around you. Let Christ in your heart to win even when others think you're losing. Proudly declare today **"I am more than a conqueror."**

Day 14

"I AM EQUIPPED FOR BATTLE"

"Put on the whole armor of God that you may be able to stand
against the wiles of the devil."

-Ephesians 6:11

Today at some point there will be something that will come against
the direction that your life is going towards. It is inevitable. In fact
there's not one person that I know that can say that their life has
been absent of trouble. Whether it is an attack from an adversary, a
trap from a wolf in sheep's clothing or even "friendly fire" from
someone close enough to you to betray your trust, it will indeed
come.

In knowing this, those of us who believe in God must know
how to respond to our enemies today and every day. We can either
surrender in defeat or equip ourselves for battle. It is noteworthy
throughout the course of time that every soldier who's gone out for
battle equipped themselves for what would lay ahead of them.
Depending on the devices available, soldiers must have on the
right garments on their feet to tread upon the terrain that they
cross. They would put on the necessary protection for the core of
their body to keep it intact. What got my attention the most is that

many soldiers will put something lastly on their head to keep the brain covered from flying weapons, bullets and such! This is powerful to see the standard of protecting the head in battle.

This very thing was discussed by Paul to the church at Ephesus as he encouraged them to put on the whole armor of God. "And take the helmet of salvation, and the sword of the Spirit, which is the word of God; praying always with all prayer and supplication in the Spirit being watchful to this and with all perseverance and supplication for all the saints (Ephesians 6:17-18)."

Taking the helmet of salvation covers the head. If your mind is covered under the knowledge that God through Christ has saved you then you can face any battle before you. Having the whole armor of God protects you from the snares of the enemy.

You may feel that one of your greatest storms is before you today. You may even be subject to attacks from the worst enemy you've ever met. The battles of this world could be overwhelming you to give up. I encourage you to let the Lord be your banner. When the Lord is your banner, you will be prepared for any attack of the enemy. With His armor, you will know just what to say and when to say it. You will be aware of where you are and where you need to be.

Today's Declaration Challenge: I challenge you to cover your head in prayer, cover your eyes in faith and guard your mouth in the words of the Lord. You don't have to fight the battle you're facing today alone. Help is on the way. You've trained too hard to give up. You've experienced too much to let the naysayers stop you. You've studied too long to turn back now. You've overcome too much to let the enemy bring you down now. This battle is not yours but with the right protection, the victory shall be yours. Declare today **"I am equipped for battle."**

Day 15

"I AM ENCOURAGED"

"Now David was greatly distressed, for the people spoke of stoning him, because the soul of all the people was grieved, every man for his sons and his daughters. But David strengthened himself in the Lord his God."

-1 Samuel 30:6

Encouragement is something that is necessary for all of us. Even the most successful people need it just as much as someone who feels like a failure. Many times we can get so wrapped up with the affairs of life that we forsake moments of taking care of ourselves.

If I never had the encouragement of my parents as a young child to sing, then I may not have continued. Many years later as I started preaching the gospel, it was that same encouragement from other family members that were blessed by the "Easter speeches" (as I would call my early sermons) that helped me continue. One truth that I've come to know is that encouragement is not validation. Encouragement comes into play when you are uplifted from a low place but validation solidifies a known truth by facts. We should never confuse the two if we can help it.

King David did not need validation but he did find himself in a place where he required encouragement. The Amalekites invaded Ziklag and burned it with fire. They had also taken captive the women and children including David's wives. Those soldiers from David's own camp spoke of putting him to death by stoning him for allowing this to happen under his watch. The Bible declares in 1 Samuel 30:6 "Now David was greatly distressed, for the people spoke of stoning him because the soul of all the people was grieved, every man for his sons and daughters. But David encouraged himself in the Lord His God."

When no one else was with him, David had enough fortitude to not let the distress he felt become the end of his story. He knew that he had to do something. He had enough tenacity to lift himself up from that low place. He used the power of self encouragement to find a place of peace with where he was and what he was presently dealing with. He didn't rely on the words of another to settle him. There were no social media outlets for him to run to for a recruitment of "likes" or persons to give him assurance that all was well. He completely had to do it himself and for himself.

Maybe you're in a similar place or position where it appears that no help is in sight. You may be facing mountains of responsibilities financially, emotionally or physically but be encouraged that God is on your side. Even when you don't feel like it, you have to command the best parts of you to live and fight on. There will be times when you don't want to, however your life depends on your declaration and your decision to press on regardless of what you see.

Are you able to encourage yourself today? Do you constantly seek out other people to do it for you? Do you know how to dig deep within and pull yourself up in low moments? Whether you're in the middle of many great successes or bound by trouble, make sure that you know how to uplift yourself before you wait on others to do it.

Today's Declaration Challenge: I challenge you to speak into yourself. Take a moment to look at the man or woman in the mirror. Speak life over yourself. Speak love, joy and peace to yourself. Before you give up, have a conversation with your inner being and call forth the greatness of the Lord within. Let the Lord fill you with his Spirit to know that where you are is not the end of your journey. Today audaciously declare **"I am encouraged."**

Day 16

"I AM HEALED"

"But He was wounded for our transgressions, He was bruised for our iniquities; the chastisement for our peace was upon Him, and by His stripes we are healed."

-Isaiah 53:5

Every day there's someone that you and I know of that is battling some form of sickness. It very well could be you in an unexpected way due to an accident externally or an internal illness. One thing is sure and that is sickness will befall us all at some point. Whether it is a physical or emotional illness, it will come our way. You could be perfectly fine to the common eye and be in the middle of a mind battle at the same time to hinder your decisions. That's an emotional illness.

Physical illnesses can happen due to any freak accident or unforeseen internal problem or imbalance that disrupts a person's normal functionality. The pathway to our healing should always start with our faith. The world had become so immersed in the sickness of sin in the Old Testament that there was a need for a healing. We needed a Savior and one to heal us from the shape that we were in. God himself recognized this and sent his messenger

Isaiah to prophecy of the one who would be our healer. Isaiah 53:5 states "But He was wounded for our transgressions, He was bruised for our iniquities, and the chastisement for our peace was upon Him and by His stripes we are healed." The foretelling of Jesus as our Savior, sets the stage for us to receive the healing power of God.

Claim your healing today. When today brings frustration and pain your way, make sure you end it with healing on your mind. In the face of sickness, you can still receive the report of the Lord that healing belongs to you.

The woman with the issue of flowing blood made a choice to be healed when she declared "If only I may touch His garment, I shall be made well (Matthew 9:21)." She made a decision to go after her healing. She internally decided that where her doctors fell short God would take up the slack. There are some cures that may come through modern medicine but as believers we believe that the ultimate healing only comes from above. Your healing may come in different ways but it will come. Let it begin in your mind.

It is also very noteworthy that every pain is not external or internal. There are some spiritual hurts and pains that need healing. As a believer or servant, it is extremely difficult to effectively serve when you're hurt by others in ministry, family or even friends. Spiritual or even church hurt is one of the worst hurts to get over but you can. By spending more time with the Lord in private, God will encourage your heart and no longer let the hurt of yesterday reside in your vessel.

Today's Declaration Challenge: I challenge you to make healing your choice. Let the love of Christ by His sacrificed life make you whole. Let the blood of Jesus cover you, your family, your resources, and connections in prayer. I encourage you to not neglect the forms of medicine that could possibly help you in the long run. God created those who created it. Be healed to exist around even your enemies. Be healed by the wounds in His side. Today readily declare **"I am healed."**

"I AM A SERVANT"

"For you, brethren, have been called to liberty; only do not use liberty as an opportunity for the flesh, but through love serve one another."

-Galatians 5:13

Servitude is a rare thing these days. It's hard for many people to remain in service to another. For the caregiver that watches an elderly person with a debilitating condition or Alzheimer's, they would tell you that they felt a calling to serve in that area of healthcare. Service comes natural for them.

For the parents of a child stricken with an unforeseen illness, they would readily testify that at no point would they leave their child helpless but rather give up their agenda to make sure that the needs of their child would be met. They too had to become servants in a way to ensure that their child's well being would remain.

This same spirit of service can be found in and out of many local church congregations around this land and abroad. Week after week, pastors, ministers, deacons, trustees, teachers, choir members, staff members, board members and doorkeepers make sure that the work of the Lord remains in and out of the walls that they are called to.

Although there are those that fully understand what service is all about, there are still others who do not. Some people feel that being a servant will make them popular or famous, which is not the case for everyone. They look at service as an opportunity to push their agenda above others. Such persons have to hear their name called or see their name in lights. Those are not true servants. I dare submit to you that character such as that is not what God's word nor Christ ever taught or desired.

In Galatians 5:13, it reads that "For you brethren have been called to liberty: only do not use liberty as an opportunity for the flesh but through love serve one another." It calls us to lovingly serve one another. Paul suggests that even in our liberty we should still choose to serve one another. In knowing that we have liberty or freedom to do what we will, we shouldn't do anything to glorify ourselves. That becomes self-service and not selfless service.

Jesus would even state in Matthew 20:27 "And whosoever desires to be first among you, let him be your servant just as the Son of man came not to be served to but to serve and to give His life a ransom for many." Great leaders are great servants. You cannot lead unless you first know how to follow or serve.

The qualities of a servant for the Lord are unique. Servants ensure that day to day operations happen with a spirit of excellence. They don't look for excuses but rather solutions. They make things happen. Servants are also wise to know that there is a time for serving and a time for instruction. Sisters Mary and Martha would experience this in Luke 10 when Jesus visited Martha's home and Mary sat at His feet to hear his words while Martha served. Jesus would tell Martha in her frustration "But one thing is needed, and Mary has chosen that good part, which will not be taken away from her (Luke 10:42)." Serve the Lord by your works and your attention to what He has spoken.

Today's Declaration Challenge: Be challenged to allow God to show you a way you can serve someone in their tough times. I encourage you to look for ways that you can go beyond yourself. I challenge you to serve God with gladness and not for attention or self-indulgent reasons. Serve to be a blessing to your family, friends and colleagues. Today declare **"I am a servant."**

Day 18

"I AM SAVED"

"But what does it say? The word is near you, in your mouth and in your heart (that is the word of faith which we preach): that if you confess with your mouth the Lord Jesus and believe in your heart that God raised Him from the dead you will be saved."

-Romans 10:8-9

Salvation is paramount for every Christian believer. It was at a very early age that I gave my life to the Lord. I remember being immensely sorrowful for all that I had ever done wrong and seeking God's forgiveness. I was led in the sinner's prayer and a prayer of salvation and I remember turning those tears of sadness into tears of joy as God gave me joy divine. I was saved.

Even though that moment brought joy and much hope, it did not remove me from all trouble. Troubles would still come but now I have Christ as my Savior to lean on. With the Lord in your life, He brings fruit to your life, which adds to the fullness of your salvation. Salvation causes you to walk a different way and move freely in the Lord.

Well in a separate moment in my childhood, my family and I journeyed to one of Florida's great beaches one summer and

I being rambunctious, decided to explore the waters. While on a circular flotation device, a wave pushed me out towards the deeps of the gulf. I clearly was too far from the shore or the calmer side of the beach to paddle back. I also was too inexperienced to swim back. As I cried out for help towards my father back on the beach, fear began to set in. What if I didn't make it? What if I drowned? I was alone and afraid.

Just when I thought there was no hope, my father (one who knew how to swim) swam out to where I was and pulled me back to the shore. I was saved. All I could do was thank my father for being there and sigh with great relief that I was still here.

As a believer, daily things will come to test your faith and your salvation no matter if you're newly converted or mature in the faith. Some tests come on jobs with underhanded coworkers, some tests happen in family units or with unfaithful friendships but keep the faith of your salvation confession. Have the kind of faith that believes that He is the Lord Jesus and that God raised Him from the dead. Have the faith that identifies Him as the Lord of your life.

It's noteworthy that some spiritual groups or affirmations will pronounce such heavy standards of salvation on its members. We see many different forms of believers today that do things differently but preach and read from the same Bible. There are some that will tell you that if you don't jump through the right hoops then you're not fully saved. That's not valid always. That's a form of tradition. Salvation comes by our confession, acceptance and belief in the Lord Jesus. He makes the change in our lives. He sets the standards for us to live and redirects our lives. He dismisses our old nature and grants us a new nature in Him. No matter what mankind may say, you still have to live in the liberty that God has given you. You have to have faith in your own salvation that will deepen your relationship with the Lord.

When you have that kind of faith, your salvation will begin to strengthen your daily walk. God the Father will keep you from the waves of trouble that seek to take you out. God will rescue you from perishing even if it's from your own actions or thoughts that led you to the place of pain. He's still saving His own. He's still keeping His own. He's still taking care of His children.

Can you witness to the power of your salvation? It's not always welcomed to testify of your salvation everywhere you go which is why the life that we now live must speak up for us before anyone hears us say that we're saved. Let your life witness to your salvation. The way we treat others should be able to show that you serve a loving, saving and forgiving God by showing those same characteristics to others.

Today's Declaration Challenge: Today let your salvation keep you from the snares of this world. Be challenged to live as Christ lived. In times of distress whisper a quick prayer to God for Him to deliver you from the perils of this world. Don't allow naysayers to push you back to the old you. That man or woman is gone. You're a new creature in Christ Jesus (2 Corinthians 5:17). Invite Christ in your heart and let him order the steps you take. Make the rest of your days the best of your days. Proudly declare **"I am saved."**

Day 19

"I AM A FIGHTER"

"Then Jacob was left alone; and a Man wrestled with him until the breaking of day. Now when He saw He did not prevail against him, He touched the socket of his hip; and the socket of Jacob's hip was out of joint as He wrestled with him. And He said, "Let Me go, for the day breaks," but he said "I will not let You go unless You bless me!"

-Genesis 32:24-26

Today you may have to fight your way through life and some things around you. You may have to fight for what you believe, what you know, your family and even your sanity. There's nothing wrong with that. It means that some days our struggles or battles are more prevalent than others.

When you stand up for what's right and stand up for others in their weakest of times, it shows maturity and growth within you. While you're on your job (that you worked hard to get) and a position that you've prayed for, there will be moments where you'll have to fight to contain your peace. Those moments will come.

Let's face it, not every day will you feel that success is on your side and that all things are going your way. It's in that moment when you do face trials and adversities that you must grab hold to what you know and fight for what you need. Truth moment: I never identified myself as a fighter but if anything or anyone came against my brothers and I, I didn't mind speaking up for them and readying myself for a fight. It just came upon me. I never sought out opportunities to fight but I would be crazy not to defend myself.

It is worth mentioning that for whatever stage we're in the middle of, life will bring resistance our way. Our fights may be different for where we are. A young college student may be fighting to meet the necessary requirements to graduate and make their family proud. The pressures to make something of yourself may be your daily struggle but keep fighting.

A husband and wife may be in a fight to make their marriage work after many battles in private but masking it publicly. That is a fight that only prayer, a new perspective and God himself can reconcile. Parents may be in a fight to raise godly children in an ungodly world. That's a fight that only will be won with love, dedication and gentle spirits.

A biblical fight happened between Jacob and a Man, who would be called out as God himself later on. Jacob was prevailing over the Man in the fight and as the day breaks the Man begs Jacob to release him in Genesis 32:26 where it states, "And He said let Me go, for the day breaks" but he said "I will not let go unless You bless me." Verse 28 of Genesis chapter 32 reads that the Man told Jacob "Your name shall no longer be called Jacob but Israel for you have struggled with God and with men and have prevailed."

Jacob knew that he had encountered someone of importance in that moment. He made a choice that he would keep fighting until he received a blessing from the Lord. The blessing would come but it also would leave Jacob with a limp for the man hit his hip socket. If you need anything in this life that you can't make it without, keep fighting for it. There's a blessing in your fight. Endure it until the end. You may come out with a limp but keep fighting. The limp will serve as a battle wound that you are a survivor. It serves as a reminder that you're strong and that you fought until the end. You may see giants before you today but keep fighting and speaking up for what you believe in. Giants (or big obstacles in your way) still fall down.

Today's Declaration Challenge: I challenge you today to fight for what's right. Fight for the greater good. Fight for your life and what you love. Fight the good fight of faith. Don't let anything separate you from your purpose. Fight for your peace. When your enemies come your way to try to bring you down, lift your voice and declare **"I am a fighter."**

Day 20

"I AM LOVED"

"For God so loved the world that He gave His only begotten Son, that whoever believes in Him should not perish but have everlasting life. For God did not send His Son into the world to condemn the world, but that the world through Him might be saved."

-John 3:16-17

Today I want you to wake up with the full knowledge that you are loved. In this world where very few people express genuine love, always know that God loves you. Love should not only be said but shown in the way that we treat each other. There's no greater expression of love than a love that is seen.

Love has a certain power if we let it in our lives. Love has the propensity of lifting us up from the lowest of places. The songwriter James Rowe would pin it best when he wrote the lines of the 1912 hymn singing "Love lifted me, when nothing else could help, love lifted me." For the writer of that song, love from the Savior reached down and picked Peter up from drowning after his "walk of faith" on the water's surface.

Love should be shown even with those that don't like us,

don't agree with us or even look like us. The opposite of love is still hate. Maybe you're in a place where you need God's love to overshadow you today or just lift you up. Maybe you've experienced the loss of a loved one or the end of a marriage or relationship that you thought would never end. If that's your story, don't let someone that wasn't able to love you, stop you from living your life. You are not defined by who left your life, you are defined by the love you still have for who remained.

Where man's love ends, God's love begins. In fact His love has been here for us before mankind could ever attempt to love one another. God loved us in spite of us. He showed His love in a sacrificial and powerful way when He gave His only begotten Son, Jesus Christ of Nazareth. "For God so loved the world that He gave His only begotten Son, that whoever believes in Him should not perish but have everlasting life (John 3:16)." For if God's love endured shame for us on Calvary's cross, we should willingly commit our ways to Him and love Him with our whole heart.

If you feel that no one loves you this day, I implore you to cancel that thought from your mind. You need to firstly and completely know how to love yourself. Love yourself in the totality of your flaws, attributes and even who you have become. Love your growth. Love the journey of your life. Love the skin you're in. Love who you are in such a great way, that you embrace the entirety of your past, present and your future.

We've seen God's love towards us every day that we live our lives by the breath that we breathe. Every day that He gives us is another chance to express His love towards someone. His word teaches that "He who does not love does not know God, for God is love (1 John 4:8)." Since we know He is love, it behooves us to give that love outwardly and watch the difference it will make in our lives.

Today's Declaration Challenge: I challenge you to love your own imperfections. Let love permit you to be a blessing to someone less fortunate than you or downtrodden in their lot. Love yourself to know what is best for you and what needs to be dismissed by you. Be wise enough to release yourself from any hurt that doesn't receive or give your love back to you. Be challenged to love so genuinely or strongly that any form of weak or fake love can't stand around you. Don't allow an old soul tie to keep you from loving yourself and letting God's love reside in your heart. Today wholeheartedly declare **"I am loved."**

Day 21

"I AM GOD'S PROPERTY"

"Nevertheless the solid foundation of God stands, having this seal:
"The Lord knows those who are His," and "Let everyone who
names the name of Christ depart from iniquity."

-2 Timothy 2:19

At the moment of our salvation, something transformative begins to happen. We transition from being sinners to new converts, to becoming adopted into the family of God. We now belong to God. Though we can still make choices on what to do for the rest of our lives and have sound decisions for our futures, we are no longer our own but rather His.

2 Timothy 2:19 which tells us "The Lord knows those who are His" is a powerful statement. In understanding that you and I as believers belong to Him, and that He knows us, that alone should essentially change our nature. It also should shape the way that we do things and conceive thoughts internally.

Young adolescents and adults are often instructed by their parents and loved ones to guard their hearts and govern their bodily actions carefully, which is rightly so. Parents and older loved ones don't do this in a demeaning way but rather a protective manner. It beseeches a young mind to pay much attention to such wisdom. You may hear this also because there will always be an influx of things that desire to overwhelm the body of believers. These things will try and make you and I pursue less than spiritual choices as long as the earth remains.

As long as we live, we are called to be God's representatives in the earth. We are His hands and His feet as my pastor, The Rev. Sean Dogan would declare. Since the Lord knows those who are His, today our thoughts should be led from a desire to accomplish goals with Him in mind. By belonging to God, He places much value in us and deems us worth keeping. I don't know about you but I'm so glad that regardless of all the crazy decisions I've made and unwise things I've done, He thinks I'm worth keeping. Since He thinks I'm worth that much, my desire should always be to represent Him. That's good news today that He knows us and values us!!

Paul wrote that we should be "living sacrifices, holy and acceptable to God which is our reasonable service. And do not be conformed to this world but be transformed by the renewing of your mind (Romans 12:1-2)." You and I have a responsibility to live our best lives. Does that mean to live in a bubble? No, not at all. It does mean that we should watchfully and carefully live in a manner that pleases God.

It is possible to belong to God and still have a fun and an

enjoyable life. It is possible to have the Lord's hand in your life and achieve dreams and goals that seemed unreachable. It is possible to worship God and still have your personal visions come to pass. Belonging to God is not the end of your life but rather the beginning of a blessed future with Him. I would rather be on His team than any other.

Today's Declaration Challenge: Today I challenge you to live as God's property. Take care of your temple (your body) by watching your actions, nutrition and physical activity. Be challenged to not conform or be shaped by this world's systems and ideals but by God's will. Live free of pressure from peers and the opinions of others but today affirm that **"I am God's property."**

Day 22

"I AM STRONG"

"Therefore I take pleasure in infirmities, in reproaches, in needs, in persecutions, in distresses, for Christ's sake. For when I am weak, then I am strong."

-2 Corinthians 12:10

There will be days and times when you will have to pronounce strength over yourself. Today might be that day. The idea of being strong rests upon a commitment to endure the weights of this world and not waiver. Real strength isn't always visible but many times it is internal.

I'll never forget the time my Marine father, was being deployed to Saudi Arabia in Operation Desert Storm, while my twin brother and I were in the 2nd grade. In that moment of his departure, I remember being sad because we would not see our dad for a while but two things happened in retrospect of that experience. The first thing that happened was that my father had to now use his training, intellect and skills in the deserts of Saudi Arabia for the duration of his deployment. The second thing that was noteworthy in my mind, was that back home my mother now had to step up and become both mother and father to three sons and make sure our lives continued to flow as it normally had.

Right before my eyes I saw strength being displayed in one of the most trying times for our family. I witnessed two individuals not live in despair or states of weakness even though they could have. They chose to live in strength. They chose to be strong.

Paul had to make a choice to be strong in a state of weakness himself. As he dealt with a thorn in the flesh, he asked of the Lord to remove it from him. God assures him that "My grace would be sufficient for you, for My strength is made perfect in weakness (2 Corinthians 12:9)."

Paul finds rest in God's grace and states in 2 Corinthians 12:10 "Therefore I take pleasure in infirmities, in reproaches, in needs, in persecutions, in distresses for Christ's sake. For when I am weak, then I am strong." Is that your affirmation today? Can you say the same even in the midst of infirmities that you are indeed strong?

Gyms all over this land are filled with persons that are strong physically. These persons have set aside time to strengthen their outer man or woman. With hard work and dedication, they will eventually see results from all of their efforts. Paul realizes that as a believer, strength comes from above even in our weakest moments. He recognizes that instead of complaining about the thorn, he finds joy in his distress to handle the thorn. A strong man handles weights, but Paul handles burdens with joy. The results produce a strong physique for the strong man but for the spiritual man, it produces a strong and mature character and faith.

Who are you being strong for? Where do you need strength today? Could it be for the peace of your family, your job or yourself? I suggest to you that any area that you need help in, God will be just that for you. He knows your struggles and your pain and the psalmist writes of God's hand saying "strong is Your hand and high is Your right hand (Psalm 89:13)." I'm so elated to know that God's strength makes itself known to us when we need it the most.

Today's Declaration Challenge: I challenge you to live in strength. With weakness in your body, be bold to declare you are strong. Even in the face of great loss and tragedy, with tears in your eyes, know that your present state is not your final condition. Be strong enough to function under attack and when traps come your way find safety in the grace of our Lord. Speak strength over your life for whatever stands against you. Today boldly declare **"I am strong."**

Day 23

"I AM REDEEMED"

"Let the redeemed of the Lord say so, whom He has redeemed from the hand of the enemy,"

-Psalm 107:2

Redemption is a precious thing to have as a child of God. It is a restorative act from a place of despair. It is when something that was once discarded as insignificant can be utilized all over again.

My case in point would be: I'm a lover and consumer of fruit juices. Those juice plastic bottles and paper containers could be viewed as useless once their emptied. Well as time would have it and advancements would come, recycling centers emerged for such materials as plastic, paper, glass etc. to be left and received for recycling later on. Essentially that glass bottle that once held soda can be utilized by an artist of glassware or art pieces.

Redemption is a beautiful thing. Not only do we visibly see it in the things that we use from day to day but we also encounter it within the kingdom of God. Have you ever been in a low place of desperation, where you didn't think or believe that you would come back from that place? If your testimony is like mine you would quickly answer yes.

I can witness that it was only the power of God in worship, the moving of God's Spirit and the fellowship of the saints that put me back to where I needed to be. I'm thankful that God knows how to redeem us from the cares of this world. My brothers and sisters, I suggest to you that your redemption should bring you from a place of testing to a place of a testimony.

The psalmist writes about those who have been redeemed by saying "Let the redeemed of the Lord say so, whom He has redeemed from the hand of the enemy (Psalm 107:2)." The writer of this psalm would give us the thought that anyone who has been redeemed from anything has a right to declare it from their lips. It's almost as if your redemption isn't complete until you're able to open your mouth and declare what the Lord has done for you.

If God's love pulled you out of the hand of the enemy, out of depression, out of the pressures of bondage and despair you have a responsibility to give Him praise. Redemption does not only bring about an outward testimony from our mouths but it should also ignite purpose to do more. It should motivate you to serve God in a more excellent way. Redemption calls you from a place of uselessness to a place of productivity.

What do you feel a strong urging to do but you haven't tapped into yet? Will you allow the ways of others to stop you from living to your fullest potential? Will you let who others remember you as stunt your growth to whom you've been called to be? Will you turn your thankfulness of being redeemed into a life of gladness and servitude towards the Father? Who do you need to redeem in your eyes that God has already given another chance to? Do you need a new start?

If you're like me, you will admit that you need God to renew, refresh and redeem some areas in your life. I'm so glad to know that no matter how washed up I may feel, God's purpose pulls me back to a place of effectiveness. I dare you to not let anything stop you from trying again, from winning again and from living again.

Today's Declaration Challenge: I challenge you to accept your redemption completely. Receive it in your heart, your mind and your body. Declare that God has done wonders for you. Proclaim like Job in Job 19:25, that you "know your redeemer lives." Let that same redemption you received work for another. You are a new creature. Today proudly declare **"I am redeemed."**

Day 24

"I AM ALIVE"

"Likewise you also, reckon yourselves to be dead indeed to sin, but alive to God in Christ Jesus our Lord."

"Let everything that has breath praise the Lord. Praise the Lord."

-Romans 6:11, Psalm 150:6

In a world where people are senselessly losing their lives to tragedies and unforeseen danger, today and every day your confession should be "Lord, thank you for my life." As you made your way out of bed, began your morning routine and set tasks for the day, cherish every moment knowing your life could have been another way.

Every day is a blessing. Every day that you inhale and exhale air is a gift from up above. When you come to the awareness and the consciousness that you are daily waking up to the gift of life and being alive, you no longer have time for detrimental matters.

As believers, we don't have to find ourselves in the midst of drama and pointless connections when we are in God. Romans 6:11 reads "Likewise you also, reckon yourselves to be dead indeed to sin, but alive to God in Christ Jesus our Lord." Paul writes from the stance that we all should eventually pronounce the end of sin and enjoy the liberty that a new life brings in Christ.

Today you may not have everything that you thought you should have or want but you have your life. You may not know everything you would desire to know but you have a mind to think and still learn a new thing. You may have lost some loved ones that were essential to your success but you still have your life. You may be lacking the funds for that great thing you've always desired to accomplish but you have your life. With your life, you have time to work to bring your dreams to pass.

Let me encourage you today, as long as you have breath in your body you've got another chance to live your best life. Thank God for where you are and as you make your way past a new plateau continually give Him glory. In fact the psalmist would write that it's a requirement for those of us that breathe to bless Him. Psalm150:6 reads "Let everything that has breath praise the Lord."

Understand this, your praise should go with you always. It should not cease. Don't let anything stop your praise. Don't let anything stop you from living. If you have to step in your prayer closet and lift up your hands in victory do it. If you have to whisper a prayer in the restroom of your place of employment, do it.

Live your life. Buy that thing that gives you much fulfillment and satisfaction. Treat yourself every now and then.

Take yourself out. Enjoy time away from the norm for a moment if you need to better yourself. Set goals for yourself. Make your living in a dignified and productive way and enjoy this life. No matter where you are today, lift your voice and thank God for your life.

It matters not if you have a lot or a little, by having your life, you have everything you need. There will always be those around you that will complain about what they don't have or what they don't need. Never let the perspectives of others deter you from enjoying the life God has given you. Where others see a complaint, you should see an opportunity to make something better. Live to live again.

Today's Declaration Challenge: Be challenged to make the most out of your journey. Life is too short to not love it while you have it. I challenge you to go after a new thing, a new business, a new relationship or connection and even a new goal. Be thankful that yesterday wasn't your last day. Where others failed, you survived with the gift of life. Today willingly declare "**I am alive.**"

Day 25

"I AM A WORSHIPER"

"But the hour is coming and now is when the true worshipers will worship the Father in spirit and truth; for the Father is seeking such to worship Him. God is a Spirit and those who worship Him must worship in spirit and truth."

-John 4:23-24

I fondly remember the excitement of going to church as a child. My home church, Fairfield United Methodist Church afforded me the opportunity to experience worship and the power of God's spirit by uplifted songs, powerful preaching and unique fellowship.

Growing up in the 1980's and 1990's, I experienced worship in a way that I always likened to be true. This was before all of the technological advances of the 21st century. There were no gimmicks or magic tricks to the church, it was simply worship. No flashing lights and smoke machines like what we see in some houses of worship of today. That same spirit of worship would mold my life profoundly to where symbols of worship would follow me home. It would not be shocking to see my brothers, cousins and I "having church" on the front steps of my grandfather's home. Worshiping God was impressed upon us to where we couldn't easily forget it.

As believers, our worship should not just be subject to our church but wherever we are and wherever we find His Spirit to be. You may face some hurdles along your pathway today but be encouraged to still worship God and watch Him go before you to handle every tough situation.

I often find myself in worship where others might least expect it. It can happen while driving (with hands on the steering wheel of course) or even in my kitchen. It can happen anywhere when I become selfless (to not focus on my problems), truthful (when I tell Him of what I'm going through) and spiritual (where I make a connection with Him in the spirit). Worship can happen at any moment.

Such an occurrence took place when the Samaritan woman came in contact with Jesus in the land of Samaria. She indeed questioned his decision to be there at the well and why he asked her for a drink of water. He let her know everything she had ever done and then she perceived Him to be a prophet. She then tried to point Him to a proper place of worship as if He shouldn't have been there. She picked up on the fact that He was a Jew and thought He should only worship in Jerusalem.

Jesus took it upon Himself to teach about worship. He informs her that worship was changing in a way. He tells her "But the hour is coming and now is when the true worshipers will worship the Father in spirit and truth, for the Father is seeking such to worship Him. God is Spirit, and those who worship Him must worship in spirit and truth (John 4:23-24)."

I choose to worship today. I worship the One that found me where I was and gave me a new reason for living. I make a decision to worship God when I pray to Him, sing a song unto the Lord, read His word and spend time in His presence. Wherever you are today don't forget to worship. Let God inside your heart and let Him do for you what He did for the Samaritan woman by making you whole. There are still great things that are only unlocked to us when we reverence God, our King in worship. Once we acknowledge God as the King of kings and Lord of lords in our lives, we can petition what we desire.

Today's Declaration Challenge: I challenge you to never lose your sense of worship. Worship the One that redeemed your life. Worship God indeed, knowing that He's in control of every avenue of your life. Worship Him for changing your direction and giving you a new life and a fresh start. As He leads you from here to there, declare boldly **"I am a worshiper."**

Day 26

"I AM BLESSED BY ASSOCIATION"

"And when they could not come near Him because of the crowd, they uncovered the roof where He was. So when they had broken through they let down the bed on which the paralytic was lying. When Jesus saw their faith, He said to the paralytic, "Son, your sins are forgiven you."

-Mark 2:4-5

In this world you may know many people but call very few of them friend. The truth of the matter is if you are blessed to have a faithful few friends hold them close. A true friend is hard to come by.

The Bible recalls in Proverbs 18:24 that "A man who has friends must himself be friendly, but there is a friend who sticks closer than a brother." This verse suggests that in order to have a friend, one must present themselves in a friendly manner.

Friendship is a two-way street. Let's face it, there will be seasonal friends that come your way and when they enter or exit you need to be confident enough to be okay with that. Just as there are seasonal friends, there will be lifelong friends that are consistent and impactful for you and your life's journey. I suggest to you that there are some blessings that only come our way based on who is connected to us.

The Bible gives us an example of such a blessed association in Mark chapter 2 when it speaks of four men carrying their paralyzed friend to a house where Jesus was preaching. The home was filled to its capacity of persons wanting to hear Jesus speak but that didn't stop them. In Mark 2:4-5 it reads "And when they could not come near Him because of the crowd, they uncovered the roof where He was and when they had broken through, they let down the bed on which the paralytic was lying. When Jesus saw "their" faith, He said to the paralytic, Son your sins are forgiven you." It would later read that Jesus commands the man to "take up his bed and go to his house and immediately he arose, took up his bed and went out in the presence of them all (Mark 2:11-12)."

I want to always have friends such as this. I'm thankful for the few friends I have that challenge my current position and help see me through it and into a blessed place. That's what real friendships do. For it was after Jesus saw what they did for him that He forgave and blessed the sick man. He saw their faith. Their faith brought about his healing. We all need people like that in our daily conversations that make us better and not bitter. That's a powerful friendship that would warrant others to pronounce a blessing over you because of the faith of your friends.

At this point in your life, ask yourself are your associations making you better or worse? Can you readily say that your friends have faith for your betterment? Are you stressed out or miserable with those close to you, due to their lack of trust and belief in you? Do you find the same level of support that you give others in return for your life? Are you always the outlet for someone else and never find them to be the same for you? Some of the most lasting connections I've ever had have been with persons that accept all of me and I do the same for them. Our lives are the better when we consistently see worth and value in each other.

Any connection that is not furthering your growth, supporting your present and forgiving of your past should not consume you today. If my friend conforms to side with my enemy when they are around each other, what kind of friend are they to me? A real friend speaks up on your behalf and guarantees that you're covered even around your enemies. In the same manner, when you have persons such as that in your life, you should do the same for them.

Today's Declaration Challenge: I challenge you to examine your associations and be sure that they are reciprocal relationships to where you can be a help to them and they can do just the same for you. I challenge you to go beyond the norm to be a help for someone in need. Let those around you see your "faith" today just as Jesus saw the faith of the four friends. Today readily proclaim that **"I am blessed by my associations."**

Day 27

"I AM BLESSED IN TRANSITION"

"Blessed shall you be in the city, and blessed shall you be in the country."

-Deuteronomy 28:3

Change happens for us every day that we live our lives. As the baby becomes a young adult and the adult reaches the pinnacle of their seasoned years, transition will take place. We see it in the workplace, when an employee with longstanding is removed or chooses to retire and the process for them adjusting to a new normal happens.

Transition is seen in our educational systems as students nervously enter halls of higher learning on their first few days of an academic year and eagerly anticipate the end of the term to graduate to the next level. We even see it in the life of believers who can quickly witness to where they were when the Lord saved them from their past, to their latter years of maturity in Jesus.

You may be in that place where you have to make great decisions or life has caused you to transition from where you used to be but you are in a prime place for God to bless you. You might say to yourself how can God do such a thing? How can I be blessed in my transition?

My brothers and sisters today there's hope from the word because we have a commanded blessing from the Lord in our obedience. When we are obedient to His word for our lives, we will still reap God's blessings no matter if we're up or seemingly down. The word reads "Blessed shall you be in the city and blessed shall you be in the country. Blessed shall you be when you come in and blessed shall you be when you go out (Deuteronomy 28:3&6)."

Now that's a commanded blessing, that even as you transition, God will bless your steps and your movements. In times of transition, doubt and fear will try to creep into your mind and make you feel that your movements are in vain. Transition sometimes will make you wonder if you're really in the right place or not and if God is truly with you or not. It's in those times that we have to trust Him the more.

God transitioned Abram in much to his surprise from his father's home in Genesis 12. It reads "Now the Lord had said to Abram: Get out of your country, from your family and from your father's house to a land that I will show you (Genesis 12:1)." I have always espoused to believe that even though Abram clearly heard from God that some small part in him was possibly apprehensive to fully trust in the plan of his transition. Abram did just what the Lord asked and his life was the better for it.

Are you in the midst of a great transition today? If you are, don't be afraid. God is with you. Let His commanded blessings take care you. If you're in the city or the field, be confident to know He's going to take care of you. God will meet your needs while He blesses your seed. That means He will take care of you and everything promised to you. Your transition is just preparation for your next place of destiny.

Today's Declaration Challenge: Be encouraged to transition in His grace and blessings today. I challenge your mind to believe that God will watch over your footsteps as you go. He will also guide you into your next place by His mighty hand. On this day definitely say **"I'm blessed in my transition."**

"I AM BLESSED BY CONFESSION"

"And Jabez called on the God of Israel saying, "Oh that You would bless me indeed and enlarge my territory, that Your hand would be with me and that You would keep me from evil, that I may not cause pain! So God granted him what he requested,"

-1 Chronicles 4:10

By this time, you've read about the dynamics in my opinion about being blessed. I do believe that God doesn't just bless us in one way and that we're blessed in different facets.

Today let's ponder the idea that we're blessed also by our confession. Confession is when we declare what's in our heart. It is also when we outwardly speak about what we need or where we are. I firmly believe in the power of speaking what I believe until I see it manifest.

Paul instructed the Corinthians to do this very thing in 2 Corinthians 4:13 "And since we have the same spirit of faith, according to what is written, 'I believed and therefore I spoke,' we also believe and therefore speak." There's power in what we say. Your words have influence. They can either make or break a situation.

When Jabez needed a change in his life, he let God know directly by his outward confession. He states in 1 Chronicles 4:10 "Oh that You would bless me indeed and enlarge my territory, that Your hand would be with me, and that You would keep me from evil that I may not cause pain!" So God granted what he requested." Talk about a confession. Can you say favor? I want that kind of confession for myself. Jabez was real with God and essentially let Him know I need you to bless me.

What blessings are you withholding from yourself by not speaking them? If we know God grants what we ask, what hinders us from asking? Could it be a lack of faith? Could it be fear of disappointment? Do we fully believe in the sovereignty of God or do we only have a small view of His power?

This is the time for bold faith. Keep speaking blessings over your life, family, resources, dreams and goals until God grants your request. Let's take on the character of Jabez in our daily walks. If you need your family members set free from bondage, speak it until you see it. If you need your territory enlarged, speak it until God grants you the creative genius to see it. If you need help for a special project that's on your heart, speak it until God sends someone your way that will be a bridge for your breakthrough.

Personally there are many things in my life that I've talked myself out of completing or even starting. Now if I was that strong enough to talk myself out of doing something, I definitely could talk myself into the blessings that are designed for me. Let's confess our heart's desire. Let's proclaim our blessings into existence.

Today's Declaration Challenge: I challenge you to be blessed by your words. Speak faith today over things that seem hopeless. Speak the favor of the Lord in your home, as you drive and as you interact with those in your careers. Speak the blessings of what you need with clarity. Let God enlarge your territory. Look for ways for God to favor you. Speak blessings over those around you. You can have what you say. Today proudly declare **"I am blessed by my confession."**

Day 29

"I AM PRAYERFUL"

"Pray without ceasing."

-1 Thessalonians 5:17

There's nothing like the power of prayer. I often remember that and find great joy in it. Prayer should be vital to the direction of our existences.

During my childhood, I remember exiting my room and as I passed the doorway of my parents' room, I noticed my mother therein. Though it wasn't unusual for her to be in her room, what she was doing was significant to stop me in my tracks. My mother was kneeling by her bedside and praying for her family. It was in that moment I gained a stronger appreciation for prayer as I heard my mother praying for her family.

Every child of God should have a prayer life. In a world where prayer isn't always received everywhere, we who believe in Christ should not let its exclusion from certain arenas cause us to exclude it from our daily walk. Prayer gets God's attention. It causes things to change. Whether it was David praying in the palace that God would forgive him or Christ Jesus praying in the Garden of Gethsemane, before sacrificing his life, we all need the power of prayer.

Prayer calms our storms. Paul would write to the Thessalonians that they should "Pray without ceasing (1 Thess. 5:17)." He would state that our prayers should not stop. We should constantly pray whether we're in the best or the worst of times. It grants a release of anything that hinders us from being our best.

If you're in a predicament that's pressing you down, before you tell social media about it, try taking it to the Lord in prayer. It's pretty odd that now we'll take to social media devices to voice the depths of our hearts before we will tell God about it. If all these technological things fail, you and I should still know how to get the right prayer request answered. It won't happen through email, inbox or direct messages but it will be in prayer to our sufficient and listening God.

Prayer connects us to an ever loving God who won't give up on us. Prayer creates a dialogue between us and God where we can tell him about our troubles and by His Spirit, He can lift the loads off of our shoulders. Prayer is not just for venting sessions but it's also for moments of thanksgiving. Prayer doesn't just unlock the door but it keeps the door open. It gives us access to the throne of God.

James wrote in his letter to those early Christians about the effects of prayer. James 5:16 states "Confess your trespasses to one another and pray for one another that you may be healed. The effective, fervent prayer of a righteous man avails much." He gives us the hope that when you pray it brings about a healing to broken places and fervent or strong prayers helps in great ways.

Let prayer be your choice today. You may be up against some intense powers and adversities. You may want to leave the very place you once stated that you were called to. You may need some time for yourself. If any of that pertains to you, go to God in prayer. Before you fall out, fall into the relief that only prayer can bring.

Today's Declaration Challenge: I challenge you today that before you give up in defeat, bow your head down in prayer. Pray for your enemies. Pray so much that your knees hurt from bearing the brunt of the weight. Let God in on your major decisions today. No matter if you're frustrated, happy, excited or sad, pray to a faithful and loving God. Today lift your voice and declare **"I am prayerful."**

Day 30

"I AM A SURVIVOR"

"We are hard-pressed on every side, yet not crushed; we are perplexed, but not in despair; persecuted, but not forsaken; struck down, but not destroyed"

-2 Corinthians 4:8-9

Only those that have been through the fires, trials and tragedies of life can make this declaration. I've noticed something from those persons on news programs that are interviewed after they've survived an unthinkable event. Survivors will quickly witness and say something like "I didn't think I'd make it but I kept going until help arrived." Only survivors can say something like that.

Survivors have a determination and perseverance that's undeniable. They have a countenance and a presence that is powerful. As you journey throughout your day, you may quickly testify that you too are a survivor from the pains of this world. Your survival may be from a sickness that you didn't see your way out of, a relationship that was abusive and terrible or an unexpected auto accident but thank God, you survived it. Beloved, trust me when I tell you, that you're in good company.

The Apostle Paul addresses this very thing with the Corinthians when he talks about them being "hard pressed on every side, yet not crushed; we are perplexed, but not in despair; persecuted, but not forsaken; struck down but not destroyed (2 Corinthians 4:8-9)." Anyone that can endure pressure, perplexity, persecution and being struck down is a survivor indeed.

Survivors have something on the inside that enables them to continue on. They have a fire that will not be put out. They have a zeal to continue on in spite of their surroundings. When you have purposed in your heart to live on, there's nothing else that needs to be said about how you'll do it but you know that you will. Survivors can receive news that appears grim and hopeless and still see life and hope on the other side. They will still believe that their story will continue.

You may be experiencing pressure to keep your sanity and peace at the hands of an antagonist but stay the course. Your friends may bring you more disappointments rather than delight but stay the course. God would not have permitted you to go through what you have unless He didn't see you coming out of it.

Many things we see before us are only temporary. If you wait them out, they'll soon pass over. If you can endure the hardships of sickness, unemployment, bad relationships and attacks you will see them no more. Your change will come if you fight on. Remember what Paul wrote when he said "For I consider that the sufferings of this present time are not worthy to be compared with the glory which shall be revealed in us (Romans 8:18)." After these trials, your glory will come and your life will continue.

Today's Declaration Challenge: I challenge you to find hope in your own story. If you overcame the pains of your past, there's peace in knowing you will survive anything in your present. Survive in the face of your opposition to let them know that you're still standing. Survive so powerfully that your enemies no longer matter to you. Put one foot in front of the other and declare today that **"I am a survivor."**

Day 31

"I AM FAVORED BY GOD"

"Now so it was that after three days they found Him in the temple, sitting in the midst of the teachers, both listening to them and asking them questions. And all who heard Him were astonished at His understanding and answers."

"And Jesus increased in wisdom and stature, and in favor with God and men."

-Luke 2:46, 47&52

Today it is my prayer that you experience and walk in the favor of God. I pray for the kind of favor that brings about a phone call of good news that you have been praying for. I pray for the kind of favor that unifies your family from a divisive state to a peaceful place. I pray for the kind of favor that puts you in positions you weren't qualified for and at tables with those you otherwise would not know.

I'm praying for favor today. I pray you experience favor that will accelerate and push your dreams and goals from the back burner to the forefront. I pray for the favor that brings your vision from months away to days away. The Merriam-Webster Dictionary defines favor as approving consideration or attention. A definition such as that is very fitting for an account with our Savior Jesus of Nazareth at the early age of 12 years old.

Jesus, his parents and a caravan of other relatives were in Jerusalem for the Passover and had begun their journey back by three days before they realized Jesus was not with them. Luke 2:46-47, 52 (NKJV) reads "Now so it was that after three days they found Him in the temple, sitting in the midst of the teachers both listening to them and asking them questions. And all who heard Him were astonished at His understanding and answers. And Jesus increased in wisdom and stature and in favor with God and men."

Jesus had the favor of God all over Him. This was the same favor that His mother had at His conception without the use of a man. This same favor kept Him from the hand of King Herod, who sought to kill Him when He was a baby. This same favor kept Him from harm in the holy city and sustained Him in the temple, without the watchful eye of His parents. It allowed Him to comprehend, answer and ask questions to great teachers and leaders of that day in the temple. It was that same favor that followed Him as He grew into adulthood and the calling that God set before Him.

Do you desire that kind of favor? Do you need the Lord to show up in a miraculous way for you? If that is your testimony I pray that you allow all that you are to come under subjection to God's Spirit. Ask what you desire from Him in prayer and listen for ways of Him to answer.

Be wise in your decisions and kind to those around you and eventually the harvest of your ways will come back around to you. Favor recognizes favor. If you're good to God and even your brothers and sisters that you see every day, that same favor will come back around and then some towards you!!

Today's Declaration Challenge: Today I dare you to pray for God's favor to rest on you. Submit your all to God and watch Him give great attention and consideration to you. Look for God to work behind the scenes for you. Be open to receive unusual kindness and divine help this day and declare **"I am favored by God."**

Day 32

"I HAVE A SOUND MIND"

"For God has not given us a spirit of fear, but of power and of love and of a sound mind."

-2 Timothy 1:7

As today started out for you, I pray you awoke with a sound mind. It's very salient that before you begin any endeavor that your mind is at peace and clear. I often share with young people when I preach on "Youth Sunday" services that "your mind is the control room of your body." It is the truth in many ways. What my mind thinks, my body will essentially follow. Every action that I've committed, originates in my head as a thought and instructions are sent to my body to carry out that command.

Every powerful move or movement that this world has ever seen started as a thought in a sound mind. Anything that can be measured as successful came from a mind that was clear of distractions and hindrances. As a believer, in order to be effective and complete your mind must be strong, clear and sound. You may be on the verge of going back to school to finish a degree or contemplating a new venture educationally but look at it with a sound mind. Pray that God will give you clarity every step of the way.

Clarity is what Paul wrote with when he spoke to his young mentee, Timothy, in the text before us today. Timothy was about to embark upon his own ministry, separate from Paul and Paul wanted him to be well equipped for the road ahead. He encouraged him in 2 Timothy 1:7 which reads "For God has not given us a spirit of fear, but of power and of love and of a sound mind." He lifts him up to know that in our flesh we may be fearful at times but that kind of fear was not given to us by God.

Do you have fear of any kind that overwhelms you from fulfilling your calling and living with a sound mind? Do you carry around fear many times in your daily walk and not realize it? Could it be because of intimidators around you and I that we fail to have a sound mind but rather a fearful one? If we are rooted in God, He gives us a sound mind to be "swift to listen and slow to speak" as James 1:19 reads. A sound mind will keep you from evil, because your thoughts are thorough and settled. Let the Lord settle your mind.

There are times that you and I will hear many voices of family and friends that will try to persuade your mind to do what they desire. There are times that you will hear so much from so many that you don't know what to think yourself. Your mind can become so clouded that even it will be hard to hear from God and understand His word. It is in those times that I recommend that you remove yourself from outside influences to better hear from God.

Today's Declaration Challenge: Be determined in your thoughts today. I challenge you to remain calm in the face of skepticism, oppression and resistance. When the conditions around you seem unnerving, put your hand on your head and pray "Lord guide and keep my mind." Don't allow what's ahead of you to cause you to make a u-turn towards your past. Move forward with clarity in your thoughts. Today confidently declare **"I have a sound mind."**

Day 33

"I AM ANOINTED"

"The Spirit of the Lord is upon Me, because He has anointed Me to preach the gospel to the poor; He has sent Me to heal the brokenhearted, to proclaim liberty to the captives and recovery of the sight to the blind, to set at liberty those who are oppressed;"

-Luke 4:18

Today I encourage you to find confidence and believe in what you are anointed to do. Once you discover what you're anointed to do (through much prayer, experience and time), you have a right and responsibility to see it manifest everywhere God leads you.

All throughout biblical scriptures you will read about many personalities from Adam to Jesus, who God anointed in their own unique way to accomplish great assignments in their lives. For every believer, God has an anointing for you. It is the anointing, that no one can easily take away from you. The anointing is an outward sign of conferring a holy office. In my opinion, the anointing that God has for you will only work for you. Adversaries and others may try their best to duplicate it but they will pale in comparison to the anointing and favor on your life.

One figure that definitely testified of the anointing on his life was King David. He declared in Psalm 23:5 "You anoint my head with oil, my cup runs over." David was so anointed that even the cup of his life ran over with the anointing of God. His life was a testament to such because it was by the prophet named Samuel that he received the mantle as king of the Israelites. He was anointed over all his father's sons and even in the face of his father that did not call him in to the meeting with Samuel. It was only after the oil didn't pour on his seven brothers that David was called forth.

His own father didn't recognize him for such a calling until then. I'm so glad that when man doesn't recognize the gifts on your life that God does. Mankind may judge you as long as they want to by your outer appearance but it is the heart that you possess that God sees. The heart makes the difference. When your heart and your abilities are postured towards God it puts you in the better position to receive the anointing of God.

Jesus went into the synagogue of Nazareth, his hometown, early in his ministry to declare himself as God's son. He did this in a bold way by reading from the book of Isaiah saying "The Spirit of the Lord is upon Me because He has anointed Me to preach the gospel to the poor (Luke 4:18a)." Jesus knew that He was anointed to do amazing things. He had every right to be in the synagogue and His presence made them aware that He was God's Son though they only remembered him as Joseph's son.

With that same power, we have to move in the spirit of God's anointing before we serve in any capacity. At the time of your belief and conversion, God called you out of a world of sin. He eventually gave you a purpose and a calling to fulfill in His kingdom here on earth. What do you feel anointed and called to do? Are you operating in that anointing? When you can identify the anointing set for your life, God will then grant you a definite door to walk into it. He will set the pathway for you to prosper in that anointing.

As a child of God, we all need the oil of His Spirit to rest on us. You may be facing giants and problems in your life but look up toward heaven and say "anointing fall on me" and let God do His best work in you. Even if you feel you are operating in a certain area of ministry and you feel there are times that ministry is not for you, you may be anointed for another significant calling. God will never anoint you to fight with another in their calling. That's not how God works. The anointing He has for you will work for you.

Today's Declaration Challenge: Be confident in what you're called and anointed to do. Be bold in the power of God's Spirit. Let his anointing fall fresh on you. Your obedience to God's calling over your life will always make you effective. You don't have to compromise your anointing for anything or anyone. Walk in your calling and proudly declare **"I am anointed."**

Day 34

"I AM GOD'S CHOICE"

"But you are a chosen generation, a royal priesthood, a holy nation, His own special people, that you may proclaim the praises of Him who called you out of darkness into His marvelous light;"

-1 Peter 2:9

We are a choosy people. Our lives are made up of choices that we made for ourselves or choices at the hand of others. Though some things are just thrust upon us, we still have many things that are ultimately left up to us to decide. My case in point: the car that you drive is your choice, the mate you have is your choice, the house you live in is your choice and even the job you work many times is your choice. Though you and I don't get the choice as to what family we were born into, we do get to choose how strong the relationship is with them.

In that same manner, today I want you to consider that you are God's choice. In fact God chose you before anyone else had an opinion of you. You belong to Him. Peter describes such an idea in 1 Peter 2:9-10a which states "But you are a chosen generation, a royal priesthood, a holy nation, His own special people, that you may proclaim the praises of Him who called you out of darkness into His marvelous light; who once were not a people but are now the people of God." What a blessed word to receive in your walk today?

Once you know God and have Christ as your savior, you'll realize that His hand has been on your life all along. You will also notice that He has ultimately ordered your steps from your beginning up until right now and that He has your best interest at heart. When you know that God called you out of darkness and into His marvelous light, you will begin to carry yourself in a different manner. You will start to gladly want to show the light of God above any form of darkness.

I've come to witness that in this world, many people claim to be chosen but yet they display elitist and condescending actions. Such behavior does not reflect a "called out of darkness" life. With that said, we who believe in God have a responsibility to present Christ in our daily walk. Since He chose us, we should always make a point to choose Him. We should always seek to bring joy to those that are downtrodden. Let humility be your guide and watch the doors and platforms that it will open for you.

In realizing today that you are God's choice, I admonish you to go after the things that He calls you to do. Believe in yourself enough to dream again. Live that "called out" life that is purposed for God's glory. Live on purpose. Choose the fruits of God's spirit above the ways of this world. I encourage you today to apply yourself again, for the things that mankind rejected you from. Find peace in knowing that He's with you. When you know that God is with you it will strengthen your ability to make great choices.

Today's Declaration Challenge: I challenge you to choose God today. Choose to live in a manner that pleases Him and not the ways of this world. Walk with the power and the authority of God in your circles of influence today. Have a boldness about yourself that will not be defeated. I dare you to be a blessing to someone else. Choose the character of God and the ways of God and watch Him set the right things in motion for you. Declare for yourself today that **"I am God's choice."**

Day 35

"I AM JOYFUL"

"Then he said to them, "Go your way, eat the fat, drink the sweet, and send portions to those for whom nothing is prepared; for this day is holy to our Lord. Do not sorrow, for the joy of the Lord is your strength."

"For His anger is but for a moment, His favor is for life; weeping may endure for a night, but joy comes in the morning."

-Nehemiah 8:10, Psalm 30:5

There's nothing like the joy of the Lord. It has the power to rest on you in a special and impactful way. I vividly recall my home church, Fairfield UMC singing a song that said "This joy I have, the world didn't give it to me and the world can't take it away." Spiritual joy has the capability to lift you up from a very low and depressed place. It will put clapping in your hands, the lifting of holy hands, running in your feet and praise from your lips. It will fill your heart with gladness and replace any form of sadness.

Having "joy" in my opinion, is a must for the child of God. It will keep a smile on your face and even give you a "holy laugh" which is like a laughter you can't explain. The children of Israel were in a predicament where they needed that kind of joy in

Nehemiah chapter 8.

The Israelites had gone and lived their lives just how they wanted to without an acknowledgement of the Lord their God. They knew about God and gone back in forth in their dedication towards God. They had all come together to hear the reading of the Book of the Law of Moses, which contained the instructions of life that God had given Moses. When Ezra finished reading, the people became sorrowful to the point of mourning and weeping. This only happened because they were living contrary to the law.

Nehemiah sought to encourage them when he saw they became sorrowful by saying, "Go your way, eat the fat, drink the sweet and send portions to those for whom nothing is prepared; for this day is holy to our God. Do not sorrow for the joy of the Lord is your strength. (Nehemiah 8:10)." He induces them to find joy in the Lord.

The word of God and also His presence should do this very thing for us. It should convict us and also bring us to a place of joy. Relief and comfort in that joy will give us strength to handle anything that comes our way. You may weep a while due to family issues, financial trouble, and even emotional distress but whatever you do, don't lose your joy. In Psalm 30:5 it reads "Weeping may endure for a night but joy comes in the morning." David spoke from his own heart and experience that no matter what you face, your joy should stay put.

Pray for the joy of the Lord to find you. Pray that His joy will lift you up out of the ashes of despair and sorrow. When you have joy it will give you "beauty for ashes, the oil of joy for mourning and a garment of praise for the spirit of heaviness as Isaiah 61:3 reads. It will allow you to take off the old clothes of depression and low self-esteem and replace them with new garments of strength, praise and thanksgiving.

Today's Declaration Challenge: I encourage you to walk, live and speak in the joy of the Lord. You may be trying to recover from a major setback but rejoice in the Lord that you have the capacity to recover. God's joy will brighten even the cloudiest of days and replace any sign of mourning. If you find joy in your favorite song, fellowship with a loved one or in quiet time with the Lord, cling to that very thing. As you journey through this day, do so declaring **"I am joyful."**

Day 36

"I HAVE FAITH"

"Now faith is the substance of things hoped for, the evidence of things not seen."

"But without faith it is impossible to please Him, for he who comes to God must believe that He is, and that He is a rewarder of those who diligently seek Him."

-Hebrews 11:1, 6

In this day and time that we live in, it is very central that you and I have faith. As believers it is one of the things that we cannot live without. In a world where society boosts having material things and possessions over anything else, you need faith to make it.

Faith will enable you to face the bitterness of a divorce, the pains of sickness or the consequences of a wayward child and not lose who you are. Faith will get you up at night to pray for a loved one going through a hardship until their deliverance comes. Faith will push you into the house of the Lord so that your spirit may be revived from the ways of this world.

The writer of Hebrews deemed faith as being necessary for every believer by stating "But without faith it is impossible to please Him, for he who comes to God must believe that He is, and that He is a rewarder of those who diligently seek Him (Hebrews 11:6)." We cannot please God without faith. Faith will keep you in a place of expectation that in every situation you face, you have a God that will see you through it.

When faith resides with us, it becomes the force that pushes us to endure to see another day. If we have "mustard seed" sized faith as Matthew 17:20 states, we can accomplish great things. We can do a lot with a little. Your faith should be the tool to propel you to your next place.

Today, even if you cannot see how things will work out, your faith will be the anchor you need. There have been many things that I did not understand how they would happen nor come to completion but I had to look through my spiritual eyes. My spiritual eyes tell me to "walk by faith and not by sight (2 Corinthians 5:7). That's the moment when I must not look at what I see in the natural but rather what I see by faith in the spiritual realm. Whether you are a mother dealing with a troublesome child, a father who's exhausted trying to make ends meet for your family or a young person seeking direction on where to go, you need supernatural faith. As a believer, you need it in your daily walk to function and know the will of the Lord for your life.

Faith trumps fear. Put your faith over your fears today. When you allow faith over fears, you can face any colossal force. You can face any devil. Faith won't allow you to walk in darkness but with God as the light of your salvation. Faith ultimately places you in a place of full reliance in God's power. It also guides your spirit in a peaceful way to persevere any storm.

Today's Declaration Challenge: Be challenged to let your faith speak up for you. Let your faith give you hope that what you see will not always be. Things may or may not be going in your favor but still you need faith to sustain you. You may be in the middle of a trying predicament but walk in faith that God will lead you out by His mighty hand. In order to handle the evils of this world, you can't do it by yourself. You can't even handle them in your own understanding but rather with a faithful heart. Having faith is not an elimination of trouble but rather strength to endure it. Declare for yourself **"I have faith."**

Day 37

"I AM NEXT IN LINE"

"Moses My servant is dead. Now therefore, arise, go over this Jordan, you and all this people, to the land which I am giving to them, the children of Israel."

"No man shall be able to stand before you all the days of your life; as I was with Moses, so I will be with you, I will not leave you nor forsake you."

-Joshua 1:2, 5

Personal testimony moment: I don't prefer to stand in long lines in grocery stores, department stores or any store for that matter if I can help it. There's something about exceedingly long lines that makes my skin boil and cause me to breakout in rashes (I'm joking). I was in a grocery store some time ago and I had a few items but the lady in front of me had a buggy with 200 items in it and then she pulled out 30 coupons!! I was outdone. Patiently I turned my head until they finished. Just as soon as they did, I stepped up and the lady turns and looks at me and says "thank you for waiting and may God bless you."

In my frustration, I was caught up by all of the items that she had that I almost missed the blessing that she pronounced towards me for being patient and waiting to be next. How many times have we missed out on something great due to our lack of patience? Patience is a disciplined characteristic. It is something that must be learned.

We see it throughout the scriptures. One instance of someone who was diligent and patient to wait their turn was Joshua. Joshua served humbly as the commander of the army of the Israelites, under Moses' leadership. Moses was not a fighter but rather a prophet. He spent his time being the one God would give instructions to while Joshua would lead the warriors and armies of Israel. They were not in competition for each other's role. They were actually in sync with one another. When Moses died, God needed another voice that He could speak to and Joshua was the right candidate. He was next in line.

In Joshua 1:5 God commissions Joshua saying "No man shall be able to stand before you all the days of your life; as I was with Moses so I will be with you. I will not leave you nor forsake you." What a word of confirmation. In knowing that God will be with you, that alone should cause anyone to move forward in the boldness of being used by God.

You may be in a position like Joshua where favor is pushing you forward in line and you're fearful of proceeding. You may be praying for change to lead you to a better place. There's good news that the same God that kept your predecessor or those that came before you, will also keep you. If you have the courage to take the first step, He'll be with you in every place that your feet touch.

Today believe God for new territories. Believe God that not only is it your time but it's your turn. Accept the plan that He has for your life. Enjoy the moment of where you have been but embrace the potential and newness for where you're going. If you always look on the level that you're on, you'll miss the greater level that lies ahead of you.

Today's Declaration Challenge: I challenge you to have enough trust and belief in God for your next place. Have faith also in the unknown insomuch that while you don't know all of the details, God knows just where you are. He also knows what you need for that moment. Your time is now. Apply for the job again. Submit the request again. Sign up for the class again. Wait patiently for God's timing to manifest and when your moment comes willingly declare today that **"I am next in line."**

Day 38

"I AM CALLED BY GOD"

"Before I formed you in the womb I knew you; before you were born I sanctified you; I ordained you a prophet to the nations."

-Jeremiah 1:5

I personally affirm that God calls everyone who believes in Him and confesses Christ as their Lord and Savior to a higher calling. I believe that He grants all of us a designated area for His kingdom, on earth while we live. The offices that He calls us to serve in may be similar but the manner in which we minister in that office is different for every believer. That means that you and I can both be called to sing in the same choir but minister in song in different sections and keys.

One thing is sure, and that is that when God has a need of you in a certain manner, He will not cease until you act out the calling on your life. Personally, I knew from the age of three that I loved to sing gospel music but when God called me into the preaching ministry, my answer and willingness to accept wasn't so quick. It was only after much prayer, dreams, visions and time alone with Him and His presence that I accepted the call to serve in the capacity such as preaching. In fact most persons that are called to preach, to teach or serve didn't do it initially because they wanted to but it was the urging of the Lord that led them that way. I've always noticed that God has a unique way of putting you in the ministry that best suits you. He does all things well!!

Such was the case with Jeremiah. God told Jeremiah "Before I formed you in the womb I knew you; before you were born I sanctified you; I ordained you a prophet to the nations (Jeremiah1:5)." God had already designed and fashioned Jeremiah's life for him before Jeremiah was aware of it. I suggest to you today that God has done the same thing for you.

He knew the roads you would take, the families you would grow up in and the desires of your heart. He not only knew your beginning or your past but also your present and your future. Yet with all of our hang-ups He still called us. Even with my attitude He still called me because He knew that I would need Him to shape it to be better than it has ever been. I'm thankful through all of my shortcomings, that He still called me.

It is noteworthy that when God calls you to live for Him; He doesn't need the approval of others to do so. He sets you apart for the role that is appropriate for your life. While mankind can confirm and esteem you, it is God that validates you. I'm so glad that no matter what I may be facing, God saw me going in it as well as coming out of it. When God calls you to something, you have to do all in your power to linger faithfully, to remain integral and committed to the mission of God. It will not be easy but there's a blessing in remaining with God. Stay with God.

What do you feel called to do? Could God be calling you to another field or branch in service? Are you currently operating in the area of ministry or place that God intends for you to be at? If you feel you are where He purposed for you to be, your story isn't over. You have a responsibility to show others coming after you the way that they should go. Each one should be able to teach one.

When you say "Yes" to the Lord, it will cost you your will for His. It will bring you to places of discomfort at times and places of much joy. It will give you peace and keep you on your toes at the same time. The calling of the Lord will inspire you to always seek His presence in all that you do.

Today's Declaration Challenge: I challenge you to be confident in your calling. Purpose in your heart to fulfill the thing God has designed you to do. Walk certainly in your calling. Stand up for what you love and believe in. Be sure in your decisions and serve faithfully knowing that if He called you to it, He will see you through it. No matter who or what you may face today declare **"I am called by God."**

Day 39

"I AM PROSPEROUS"

"Beloved, I pray that you may prosper in all things and be in health, just as your soul prospers."

-3 John 2

Today it is my prayer that prosperity finds you in every way of your life. Many times, I believe in this world and day that we live in, that prosperity has only been lifted in one light for so long that it has received a bad reputation. Prosperity should not only be viewed from the stance of money. That's only one side of it. Due to the extravagance of certain persons in the world and the church we have shied away from its full context.

3 John 2 reads "Beloved, I pray that you may prosper in all things and be in health, just as your soul prospers." John writes from the premise that prosperity would be evident in "all things" or all areas of our lives that we desire to see it. I interpret that to mean even my soul (my inner-self) prospers. How so? Well daily when I commune with God in prayer and meditation of His word, I'm building my faith and my soul to a greater place. Not only does my soul prosper but my body prospers as well. My body prospers when I exercise my temple and take care of my body as a vessel

and monitor what foods I consume and intake. I can also have prosperity in my mind and my actions. Psalms 1:30 reads "And whatever he does shall prosper." I pray that kind of prosperity for your life today.

I want prosperity all around my very being. That alone should change my actions, which are initiated in my mind, to also prosper even the more. I pray that the works of your hands prosper. As you put your hand to work on anything, that God would grant productivity and much fruit from your labor.

Every fruit tree that ever thrived has a mandate to bear fruit. That is the assignment of that tree every harvest season. If the fruit tree does not produce any fruit, it essentially is of not avail to the one who owns it and even is deemed useless. When fruit is seen from the branches it's a sign that prosperity reigned from the seed that went into the ground, to the water that nourished it, to the branches and limbs that matured and to the finished product of fruit to be plucked. If you're not bearing fruit in the thing that you set out to do today, then prosperity will not come.

If you feel that you need prosperity in your life, pray that God would give you a creative idea or a new thought to always prosper. Pray that He will allow you to be wise to seek after better provisions. With discipline, hard work and dedication, God can send everything you need and then some. When you seek after God, he will cause you to prosper. King Uzziah did this very thing during his reign and in 2 Chronicles 26:5 reads "He sought God in the days of Zechariah, who had understanding in the visions of God; and as long as he sought the Lord, God made him prosper." I want that kind of prosperity that as long as I seek after God, he makes prosperity follow me.

I pray that you will have prosperity in your associations and the people that you're connected to. If you're not building anything with the ones you're with, you're only wasting your time. Build something great today. Let your connections produce much fruit in unity with one another. Prosper in your entire being.

Today's Declaration Challenge: I challenge you to walk in the prosperity that God has assigned to your life. Let God overshadow you with an insightful idea to take care of your health, your mind, relationships and the works of your hands. I pray for that prosperity would find you in your resources and that your vats would overflow. Today declare **"I am prosperous."**

"I AM THANKFUL"

"In everything give thanks, for this is the will of God in Christ Jesus for you."

-1 Thessalonians 5:18

Today and everyday should be a day of thanksgiving for you. The very fact that you're still breathing and living is enough to bless His name. The fact that you have an opportunity to live in this day is a blessing in itself and it is another chance to do mighty things.

I remember when I was a child that my family would sit down at the dining room table together and have breakfast on Sunday mornings and dinner later that day. Before we could grab the fork and partake in the macaroni and cheese, green beans, or rice and gravy we firstly had to bow our heads as my father led us in prayer. It was a prayer of thanksgiving for yet another opportunity to have nourishment for our bodies. It was a prayer from a grateful heart.

This same spirit of thanksgiving should go with you as believers, as you go about your day. As you spend resources on things that you need and desire, be thankful that you were in the position to buy what you desired, for it could have been another way. As you worship in sanctuaries or wherever you may be, you should still be thankful. We should never enter a place or moment of worship and not thank God for what He's done for us to be able to worship. When some countries outlaw religious freedoms and the choice to worship God, we should always be thankful for the freedoms to bless our God.

The psalmist declares that we should "Enter into His gates with thanksgiving, and into His courts with praise. Be thankful to Him and bless His name (Psalm 100:4)." It's a privilege to worship our Father in Heaven. It's a blessing to be given abundant life through Christ Jesus. It's an even deeper joy to find comfort and peace through God's Holy Spirit.

A man stricken with leprosy understood this all too well when he met Jesus. This man and nine other lepers were outside of a village when He came by and they cried out to Him "Jesus, Master, have mercy on us! So when He saw them, he said to them, "Go show yourselves to the priests," And so it was that as they went, they were cleansed. And one of them, when he saw that he was healed, returned and with a loud voice glorified God (Luke 17:13-15)." This man had an attitude of gratitude. As you journey from here to there, can you say the same for yourself? Have you witnessed your breakthrough and in turn gave God the glory with thanksgiving?

Today you may not feel that you have a reason to be thankful.

You may feel that there are more things stacked against you than being for you. You may have lost more than what you gathered and now you doubt your purpose to go on. I implore you to ponder not on the things that are negative but let positivity find you today. Sometimes you have to be thankful for what you don't have. Yes, for what you don't have, because it just may be that God didn't design that thing for your life. Sometimes you have to be thankful for who left your life, had they not left you, you would not know how strong you were without them. Some places had to fall apart for you to be assigned to new territories and platforms in life.

As you've journeyed through these forty days of *"Self-Declarations,"* I pray that something has provoked insight and awareness of how strong you really are. In a world filled with validation (sometimes falsely) through friends and social media platforms, Christian believers should always find confidence and validation in whom God has made you to be. I pray that you finish this devotional enlightened in the gifts that you already possess and the courage to seek God for a greater anointing and calling.

Today's Declaration Challenge: I challenge you today in a unique way. Before you complain, I challenge you to let thanksgiving come from your heart. Thankfulness will change your perspective. It makes you view things from a better vantage point. Thank God for whom you are. Thank God for where He has placed you. Thank Him for what you have inside. For if you lose your outer possessions, if He is in your heart, you will never lack again.

Thank God for your struggles, successes, for they all equipped you to be wiser and stronger. Thank God for those that will walk this journey with you, in a world where consistency many times is lacking. Thank Him for your life. It may not be what you thought it would be but it is yours.

You have the power to forge your pathway to victory. You have the choice to live as His word instructs. Thank God for a mind and mouth to bless His name. Walk in your God-given identity. Because He is the Great "I AM" you are what you say and what you believe. You are who He says you are. You can do what He says you can do and you can have what He says you can have. Today and for the rest of your days proudly declare **"I am thankful."**

.

ABOUT THE AUTHOR

Derrell L. Dean, is a licensed minister of the gospel, singer and musical director at Long Branch Baptist Church in Greenville, South Carolina. He holds degrees from Spartanburg Methodist College and Anderson University. He resides in the Anderson County Area of Upstate, South Carolina with his family.

For book presentations or additional info, please email thadeanslist22@gmail.com.